SMALL CHANGE

SMALL CHANGE

Why Business Won't
Save the World

MICHAEL EDWARDS

Berrett–Koehler Publishers, Inc.
San Francisco
a BK Currents book

Berrett-Koehler Publishers, Inc., 235 Montgomery Street, Suite 650, San Francisco, CA 94104-2916 • Tel: (415) 288-0260 • Fax: (415) 362-2512 • www.bkconnection.com

ORDERING INFORMATION

QUANTITY SALES. Special discounts are available on quantity purchases by corporations, associations, and others. For details, contact the "Special Sales Department" at the Berrett-Koehler address above.

INDIVIDUAL SALES. Berrett-Koehler publications are available through most bookstores. They can also be ordered directly from Berrett-Koehler: Tel: (800) 929-2929; Fax: (802) 864-7626; www.bkconnection.com

ORDERS FOR COLLEGE TEXTBOOK/COURSE ADOPTION USE. Please contact Berrett-Koehler: Tel: (800) 929-2929; Fax: (802) 864-7626.

ORDERS BY U.S. TRADE BOOKSTORES AND WHOLESALERS. Please contact Ingram Publisher Services, Tel: (800) 509-4887; Fax: (800) 838-1149; E-mail: customer.service@ingrampublisherservices.com; or visit www.ingrampublisherservices.com/Ordering for details about electronic ordering.

Berrett-Koehler and the BK logo are registered trademarks of Berrett-Koehler Publishers, Inc.

Printed in the United States of America

Berrett-Koehler books are printed on long-lasting acid-free paper. When it is available, we choose paper that has been manufactured by environmentally responsible processes. These may include using trees grown in sustainable forests, incorporating recycled paper, minimizing chlorine in bleaching, or recycling the energy produced at the paper mill.

LIBRARY OF CONGRESS CATALOGING-IN-PUBLICATION DATA

Edwards, Michael, 1957–
Small change : why business won't save the world / Michael Edwards. — 1st ed.
   p.   cm.
Includes bibliographical references and index.
ISBN 978-1-60509-377-2 (pbk. : alk. paper)
1. Social responsibility of business. 2. Nonprofit organizations—Management.
3. Social change—Economic aspects. I. Title.
HD60.E335 2010
361.7'65—dc22

2009040690

First Edition

15 14 13 12 11 10 10 9 8 7 6 5 4 3 2 1

Book design and project management by Valerie Brewster, Scribe Typography.
Copyediting by Elissa Rabellino. Proofreading by Don Roberts.
Index by Stephanie Maher Palenque.
Author photo by Newscast/Third Sector magazine www.thirdsector.co.uk.

Contents

Preface

In 2007, I experienced one of those fork-in-the-road moments that seem to occur when you least expect them. It was another day at the office, sifting through e-mails in the Ford Foundation's glass palace in Manhattan, where I worked as one of the organization's six directors. As usual, half of my inbox was filled by advertisements for books, conferences, and consultants promising to solve society's problems by bringing the magic of the market to nonprofits and philanthropy—the masters of the universe, it seemed, also wanted to be saviors of the world—and the other half was filled by complaints from those experiencing the negative consequences of doing exactly that. Among the latter were nonprofit organizations that couldn't get support because their work didn't generate a "social return on investment," community groups forced to compete with each other for resources instead of collaborating in common cause, foundation staff members alarmed about chief executives recruited from business with no experience in philanthropy or any other work for social change, and activists who felt passed over by a new generation of Samaritans who stopped to calculate how much money they would make before deciding whether or not to help.

The encroachment of business into politics, education, health care, and the media had been proceeding apace for twenty years or more, but this was different; this time it was personal, because it affected a lifetime's work in which I was directly involved. I had spent three decades in Oxfam, Save the Children, the World Bank, and the Ford Foundation trying to promote a strong *civil society*, which is another name for the nonprofits, social movements, and citizens' groups of many different kinds that have been a pivotal force for good, from the struggle against slavery to pro-democracy demonstrations in Iran. Faced by a tsunami of pro-business thinking that seemed to threaten the values and independence of these groups, what was I to do—keep quiet and go with the flow, or speak up and hope to influence the conversation going forward?

It suddenly struck me that this was more than a simple clash of cultures—it had potentially profound implications for the success of our efforts to transform the world in the image of love and justice. And in the rush to embrace new approaches to philanthropy, some very important older questions were in danger of being buried under hype and adulation—questions of deep social change and social transformation, of democracy versus plutocracy, and of people's willingness to work together on common problems as full and equal citizens, not as clients or consumers.

Therefore, I decided to take a closer look at this phenomenon, and at a stroke turned my gentle transition out of the Ford Foundation into an uncomfortable yearlong effort to raise some difficult and, to some, unwelcome questions. Because nobody wants to bite the hand that feeds them or seem out of step with the latest fashions of the funders, this debate lies largely hidden beneath the surface, which makes it much more difficult to identify when business thinking can help social change and when it can't. My aim in this book is to bring these questions out into the open so that they can be properly discussed, and to show why everyone should be concerned about them, not just nonprofit and philanthropy professionals. I don't want businesses

and the superrich to abandon their social conscience, but I do
want them to develop more humility and appreciation for the
complexity of the tasks that lie ahead when using business thinking to advance social change. Otherwise, the hype surrounding
this phenomenon may divert attention from the deeper changes that are required to transform society, reduce decisions to an
inappropriate bottom line, and lead us to ignore the costs and
trade-offs involved in extending business thinking into philanthropy and civil society. I'm concerned that questions like these,
and the evidence that underpins them, are not being given a fair
hearing, and I want to provoke a conversation in which all the
different positions can be aired. After all, this is the only way
that new ideas can be tested and reshaped so that they can ful-
fill their true potential, even if it turns out to be less significant
than their proponents often claim.

Some of my job has already been accomplished for me by the
biggest financial crisis to hit the world since the Great Depres-
sion, a traumatic event that has thrown cold water over claims
that markets always regulate themselves, that business protects
the public good, and that nonprofit groups must learn transparency and accountability from Wall Street's paragons of efficiency. At a time when business cannot even fix itself, one wonders
why anyone should believe that it can fix the rest of society and
its institutions. With America having lost its economic senses
under its first MBA president, George W. Bush, and started to
regain them under the community organizer who replaced him,
Barack H. Obama, it seems appropriate to ask whether America
or any other country will be better placed to solve its problems
through the application of more business thinking.

Don't get me wrong. I don't say this because I am anti-
business or because I don't like or admire the example set by
Bill Gates and other billionaires. Any successful recipe for

social transformation must include a well-functioning market economy that creates wealth—broadly distributed throughout the population—and fosters technological innovation, directed at socially useful ends. When business puts its own house in order in this way, it can have an enormously positive impact by increasing the social and environmental value of the goods and services it produces, improving the quantity and quality of the jobs and incomes it creates, and acting as a good corporate citizen—which means paying taxes, obeying regulations, ending monopolies, and removing lobbying from politics. That's a very important point: It has always been civil society and government that have pressed businesses to do these things; and to exercise their influence effectively, both government and civil society need to be strong and independent. Only then can they exert sustained pressure for accountability and act from a different set of values and priorities. Otherwise, "organized greed always defeats disorganized democracy," as Matt Taibbi puts it.[1] It's the difference that *makes* the difference to society. In fact, real transformation will occur when business behaves more like civil society, not the other way around.

The problem comes when businesses and markets undertake tasks for which they are not well designed—like rebuilding the cohesion of communities, strengthening the ways in which people care for each other, and pushing for fundamental changes in the economic system itself. Remember the old joke about the European Union that puts the British in charge of the food instead of the French, the Germans in charge of the entertainment instead of the Italians, and the Italians in charge of the administration instead of the Germans? It's politically incorrect, I know, but (speaking as a Brit) still pretty accurate. Expecting price competition, the profit motive, short-term deliverables, and supply-chain control to bring about a world of compassion and solidarity is, to say the least, a little strange. You wouldn't use a typewriter to plow a field or a tractor to write a book, so why use markets where different principles apply?

Business can certainly help to extend access to useful goods and services, and for that we should be grateful, but claims that business will save the world are a dangerous case of hubris. Social change requires an orchestra of instruments with a democratic conductor, not a single, dominant brass section constantly playing its own monotonous tune. By exaggerating the benefits of business thinking in the social sectors, we might unwittingly deflect attention away from the changes that are necessary in core business practices *and* dilute the transformative potential of civil society and government. And what would be the result of that? Small change—limited advances in society *as it is*, not as it could be if we summoned up the courage to confront the deeper problems and inequalities that capitalism creates. Why settle for small change when much greater possibilities lie within our grasp?

Despite these strictures, the business-is-best philosophy remains a powerful and seductive hook. It promises to supply a new magic bullet that removes the messiness of social change, and a route to doing good for others while doing well for yourself without any of the sacrifices that have been necessary for progress in the past. That's an attractive proposition, and also a dangerous mirage. Can we compete ourselves into a more cooperative future, or consume our way to conserve the planet's scarce resources, or grow our way out of deep-rooted poverty and oppression, or fight our way to peace? Such ideas are disingenuous at best and dishonest at worst. As I hope to show in the pages that follow, the claim that business thinking can save the world is a convenient myth for those who occupy positions of great wealth and power; and the constant celebration of rich and famous individuals is a dangerous distraction from the hard, public work of finding solutions, all of us together.

There are four key points in the argument I am going to make:

First, neither philanthrocapitalism, which I define in chapter 1, nor transformative approaches to social change are monolithic. Both contain many different strands, and they engage and overlap in the middle, sometimes with positive effects and sometimes not. These various strands and hybrids have different costs and benefits, so rather than tilting at windmills by writing off one approach *or* the other, it is more useful to identify where business thinking can advance social change and where it can't, separating out the use of business tools from the underlying ideology of the market. This is the subject of chapter 2, though it is easier said than done, given the wide variety of terms that are used in this debate and the absence of any consensus about what they actually mean.

Second, the hype that surrounds philanthrocapitalism runs far ahead of its ability to deliver real results. There is little hard evidence that these new approaches are any better at reducing poverty and injustice than the governments, foundations, and civil society groups that have been working away more quietly in the background for a generation and more. Yes, they get much-needed drugs, microcredit loans, solar-rechargeable light bulbs, and the like to people who really need these things, but they don't change the social and political dynamics that deny most of the world's population the hope of a decent life. Chapter 3 reviews this evidence and looks at the impact of philanthrocapitalism on people's access to useful goods and services, on the strength of civil society, and on national indicators of poverty and health.

Third, among the reasons for these disappointing results, one seems especially important: the conflicts and trade-offs that exist between business thinking and market mechanisms on the one hand, and civil society thinking and social transformation on the other. Chapter 4 explores these conflicts in some detail, paying particular attention to the damage that is done when a radically different logic is applied to civil society as the crucible of social movements and democratic politics. There have always been areas of life that we deliberately protect from the narrow calculations of competition, price, profit, and cost—such as our families and community associations—but in the rush to privatize and commercialize *social* action and activity, there is a danger that these firewalls will be forgotten.

Fourth, the increasing concentration of wealth and power among philanthrocapitalists is unhealthy for democracy. When the production of public goods like health and education becomes the province of private interests, fundamental questions of accountability apply. Why should the rich and famous decide how schools are going to be reformed, or what kinds of drugs will be supplied at prices affordable to the poor, or which civil society groups get funded for their work? "I remember a day," lamented Robert Reich in *American Prospect Online*, "when government collected billions of dollars from tycoons like these, and when our democratic process decided what the billions would be devoted to . . . I don't want to sound like an ingrate or overly sentimental, but I preferred it the old way."[2] He has a very important point. Weak accountability is the Achilles' heel of all systems for financing social change—new or old, public or private—and chapter 5 explores how to deal with this problem and reconfigure philanthropy so that it can be more useful to long-term social transformation.

One clear message emerges from these four points: Social transformation is not a job to be left to market forces or to the whims of billionaires. Perhaps if we supported the energy and creativity of millions of ordinary people, we could create a foundation for lasting progress that will never come through top-down planning by a new global elite, however well intentioned. When this principle is accepted and philanthropy is reconfigured to be less technocratic and more supportive of people's own self-development efforts, then change will come— larger than we can control, quicker than we can imagine, and deeper than we could ever hope for by reducing everything to market forces. So let's begin.

CHAPTER ONE

Irrational Exuberance

The Rise of "Philanthrocapitalism"

$

I t is six o'clock on a Saturday afternoon, and the Swan Lake Fire Department Ladies Auxiliary is cleaning up after its latest community rummage sale. Not much money changed hands today, but plenty of warm clothes did, much needed with the onset of winter in this upstate New York town. Prices varied according to people's ability to pay, and those who couldn't pay at all—like the mother who brought all her money in dimes, quarters, and pennies inside a plastic bag—were simply given what they needed, and driven home to boot. "Imagine what this would have cost me at Walmart," she told her driver.

In some ways, there is nothing special about this story, which is repeated a million times a day in civil society groups that act as centers of solidarity and sharing. In another sense, it is profoundly important, because it represents a way of living in the world that is rooted in equality, love, and justice, a radical departure from the values of competition and commerce that increasingly rule our world. It is not that the members of the Ladies Auxiliary are free from concerns about money and what things cost—like everyone else, they have to make a living and raise funds to support their work, and they keep meticulous accounts. But when it comes to their responsibilities as citizens, they play by a different set of rules, which are grounded in rights that are universal, not restricted by access according to one's income; they recognize the intrinsic value of relationships that can't be traded off against production costs or profit; and they live out philanthropy's original meaning as "love of humankind." Over many generations, community groups and social movements have protected these principles in their work to attack discrimination and injustice, alleviate poverty, and protect the natural world.

Across the universe, meanwhile, a very different form of philanthropy is taking shape. It has been nicknamed *philanthrocapitalism* by Matthew Bishop and Michael Green[1], and its followers believe that business thinking and market methods will save the world—and make some of us a fortune along the way. Bobby Shriver, Bono's partner in the Red brand of products, hopes that sales will help "buy a house in the Hamptons" while simultaneously swelling the coffers of the Global Fund to Fight AIDS, Tuberculosis and Malaria.[2] Larry Ellison, who founded Oracle, thinks that "the profit motive could be the best tool for solving the world's problems, more effective than any government"[3]—until government has to bail you out, of course, as it did for large swaths of American finance and industry in the aftermath of the financial crash in September 2008.

"If you put a gun to my head and asked which one has done more good for the world, the Ford Foundation or Exxon," says Charles Munger, vice chair of Berkshire Hathaway, "I'd have no hesitation in saying Exxon,"[4] though I can't think of any oil spills that my old employers have dumped into the Pacific. "This," says Jeff Skoll, who co-created eBay, "is our time."[5] There are philanthrocapitalists outside the United States, too, like Carlos

Slim, the owner of most of the Mexican economy; Nandan Nilekani, of Infosys in India; and Shi Zhengrong, of Suntech Power in China, who are all "hyper-agents," according to Bishop and Green, smashing through the barriers that have obstructed previous efforts to solve global problems. In this book, I won't be focusing on non-U.S. examples like these because so little rigorous information is available on their efforts, but it is clear that the influence of philanthrocapitalism is spreading from the United States to other parts of the world, just as in earlier generations of philanthropy. The four richest people in the world are philanthrocapitalists—Bill Gates, Warren Buffett, Carlos Slim, and Larry Ellison, with combined assets of $135 billion, more than the gross domestic product of some of the world's most populous countries, including Nigeria and Bangladesh.[6] Not all philanthrocapitalists are rich (we'll meet some of them in chapter 2), and not all rich philanthropists subscribe to these methods and approaches, but the basic message of this movement is pretty clear: Traditional ways of solving social problems do not work, so business thinking and market forces should be added to the mix.

Actually, these traditional ways, like the Ladies Auxiliary and social movements dedicated to human rights, have often worked, though imperfectly, and if we gave them more support and recognition, they could work even better—but that's not what the philanthrocapitalists want to hear. Instead, "the real scandal," says Harvard's Michael Porter, "is how much money is pissed away on activities that have no impact. Billions are wasted on ineffective philanthropy."[7] "Charities have failed for decades to deliver . . . do we want to continue with the status quo or apply some fresh, *inherently efficient* [my italics] and potentially very effective thinking to find new solutions?"[8] This statement comes from Kurt Hoffman, director of the Shell Foundation, in

a letter to the *Guardian* in London, though I could have picked
from any number of statements that are constantly repeated as
though they represent a simple and straightforward truth. In
fact, if I had a dollar for every time someone has lectured me on
the virtues of business thinking for foundations and nonprofits,
I'd be a philanthropist myself.

This is a very odd way to talk about groups that have cared
for the casualties of every crisis and recession for a hundred
years or more, kept communities together in the good times and
the bad, brought democracy alive in places very large and very
small, protected the environment from continuous corporate
degradation, pushed successfully for the advancement of civil and women's rights, and underpinned every successful social
reform since slavery was abolished. As far as I can tell, the people who make such statements have never worked in groups like
these, nor have they studied the achievements and history of civil
society organizations, nor have they experienced the difficulties
of tackling power and inequality on a shoestring and in the face
of constant opposition. On these grounds, maybe community
organizers should go work for Lehman Brothers.

Come to think of it, that's not such a bad idea: It might have
saved us from the colossal mismanagement and risk taking by
banks and hedge funds that led to the financial crisis—companies that were so successful and well managed that, like Lehman
Brothers and its foundation, they collapsed overnight, leaving
hundreds of nonprofits to face financial ruin—or it might have
spared us Bernard Madoff with his massive Ponzi scheme, who
defrauded Jewish charities of huge amounts of money and caused
whole philanthropies like the JEHT Foundation to vanish without a trace.[9] "In investment banking, it is taken for granted that
decisions about how to use capital are based on rigorous research
into performance," say Bishop and Green in their love poem to

philanthrocapitalism; or as we now know, such decisions could be based on raw speculation at everyone else's expense. What is "inherently efficient" about business thinking and the market? That's just ideology—pure, simple, and absolutely incorrect.

Not all philanthrocapitalists talk or feel this way, but the mix of arrogance and ignorance revealed in these quotations sure takes some explaining. What lies behind the rise of this phenomenon? The philanthrocapitalists are drinking from a heady and seductive cocktail, one part "irrational exuberance," as Robert Shiller puts it,[10] that is characteristic of market thinking; two parts believing that success in business equips them to make the same impact on society at large; a dash or two of the excitement that accompanies any high-profile new solution; and an extra degree of fizz from the oxygen of publicity that is created when philanthropists get the chance to mix with the world's richest and most famous people. "The new rich have often made their money very fast, and get intoxicated by their own brilliance into thinking that they can quickly achieve results in the non-profit sector. They forget that their success may be due to luck, and that the non-profit sector may be far more complex than where they have come from," says Mario Morino, head of Venture Philanthropy Partners, in a welcome dose of common sense.[11]

Shiller used the word *irrational* in the title of his famous book for a very good reason, since he knew that stock market bubbles and corrections are caused less by facts and fundamentals than by a popular consensus that becomes disconnected from what is happening on the ground. In similar fashion, the philanthrocapitalists have latched on to something potentially important—that business and the market can have more social impact—but have become so caught up in the buzz surrounding their ideas that they are ignoring the costs of what they are recommending and exaggerating the benefits.

The advance of capitalism brings many material and technological rewards, but it also dismantles the social ties and sense of common purpose that are essential to healthy and well-functioning societies; and in its present form, it promotes inequality and individual alienation. The philanthrocapitalists see more capitalism as the answer to the problems that capitalism has already created, but is this going to be enough? Especially at times of economic crisis, questions are always asked about the undue influence of businesses and wealthy individuals, the encroachment of the market into every aspect of our lives, and the erosion of older traditions of service and civic engagement. It is no coincidence that discussions of Bill Gates's ideas on "creative capitalism" have taken off just when conventional capitalism is experiencing such a loss of public trust. To prosper in the future, capitalism must be the servant, not the master, of democracy and the public good. That will require more government and civil society influence over business, and not the other way around: more cooperation, not competition; more collective action, not individualism; and a greater willingness to work together to change the fundamental structures that keep most people poor so that all of us can live more fulfilling lives.

The tide of public opinion in many countries is already turning back toward the benefits of strong government, market regulation, democratic accountability, and civil society activism (whether it stays there is, of course, another matter). High levels of grass-roots participation in Barack Obama's presidential election campaign were, perhaps, a harbinger of things to come, as civil societies begin to recover their sense of purpose and self-confidence. If these trends continue, philanthrocapitalism will face increasing questions about its relevance and reach—most important, does it actually work? Can these new approaches transform societies, or do they simply treat the symptoms of social problems in more efficient ways?

Philanthrocapitalism vs. Social Transformation

"Since 2005, commitments made through the Clinton Global Initiative (CGI) have already affected more than 200 million lives in 150 countries." In Asia alone, "more than 3.5 million people will gain greater access to health services, an estimated 715,000 children will benefit from better education opportunities, over 260,000 adults will learn new job skills, over 250,000 girls and women will be empowered with better opportunities for sustainable livelihoods, nearly 24,000 hectares of forest land will be protected by empowering local residents to manage their own natural resources, the equivalent of more than 40,000 tons of CO_2 emissions will be cut, and over 700,000 people will better learn to cope with environmental stress and natural disasters."[12]

These statistics, taken from the CGI Web site, which acts as a clearinghouse for many business-savvy philanthropists and *social entrepreneurs* (defined in chapter 2), say little about the quality and sustainability of the improvements that are claimed, but they are undeniably impressive. There is justifiable excitement about the possibilities for progress in global health, agriculture, and access to microcredit among the poor that have been stimulated by investments from CGI members, the Gates Foundation, and others. This kind of work—using business and the market to get socially and environmentally useful goods and services to more poor people—has become the largest and most visible project of the philanthrocapitalists over the last five years. As Pierre Omidyar, one of the founders of eBay, puts it, you can begin by investing $60 billion in the world's poorest people "and then you're done!"[13]

Well, not quite, Pierre. New loans, seeds, schools, and medicines are certainly important, but there is no medicine that can combat the racism that denies land to *dalits* (or so-called untouchables) in India, no technology that can deliver the public health systems required to combat HIV, and no market that can reorder the dysfunctional relationships between different religions and other social groups that underpin violence and insecurity. And that's the crucial point. Philanthrocapitalism may well produce a vaccine against malaria, but there's no vaccine against greed, fear, poverty, inequality, corruption, lousy governance, personal alienation, and all the other things that plague us. Few areas of business expertise translate well into the very different world of complex social and political problems, where solutions have to be fought for and negotiated—not produced, packaged, and sold. And, so far at least, there aren't many philanthrocapitalists who are prepared to invest in the challenges of long-term institution building, the deepening of democracy, or the development of a different form of market economy in which inequality is systematically attacked.

In most of the literature from philanthrocapitalists, the goal is saving lives, or promoting access for lower-income groups to goods and services that are productive and beneficial. "The Gates Foundation is seen as a venture capitalist," says Erik Iverson, the foundation's associate general counsel. "In return, what we want is lives saved."[14] Capitalism is philanthropic, says Matthew Bishop, because "sooner or later everyone benefits through new products, higher quality and lower prices."[15] As Jacqueline Novogratz concludes, "We should see every poor person on the planet as a potential customer"[16]—not exactly an inspiring vision to get you out of bed, but entirely logical for business.

Staying alive is certainly a necessary condition for social transformation, but it is hardly sufficient for living a life that is fulfilling, loving, and productive, and neither is increased consumption. That level of fulfillment requires changes in systems and structures, institutions and relationships, and norms and values, so that everyone can participate fully in the benefits of social, economic, and political life—and care for themselves, each other, and the planet in the process. And completing this job rests on much more than market forces. Philanthrocapitalism focuses on building up the health, skills, and assets of individuals, and I have some sympathy for this approach, which is born out of a desire to avoid the paternalism that infects traditional philanthropy and foreign aid. For those who benefit, it builds security and self-confidence, and enables people to make their own choices about how they want to spend their money and participate in society.[17]

But the problem is that this approach can only ever reach part of the population (usually the already better-off), because there will never be enough money in the system to get services to everyone who needs them on a one-by-one basis; it often imposes hidden costs on some members of society at the expense of many others (especially the less powerful and women, whose workload is often increased); and it leaves the structure of economic, social, and political life largely unchanged, thereby maintaining or increasing inequality even if absolute poverty goes down. If you wait to tackle injustice and discrimination until everyone has more assets, it will already be too late, since as history shows, economic growth rarely removes these problems by itself. Sadly, deep-rooted patterns of greed, corruption, racism, sexism, homophobia, and hatred do not disappear as incomes and other assets grow, so unless philanthrocapitalism digs more deeply into the fabric of social change, it is in danger of replicating, not transforming, existing patterns of power and inequality, even if more people have access to the loans, medicines, tools, and textbooks that they so desperately need.

"We literally go down the chart of the greatest inequities and give where we can effect the greatest change," says Melinda Gates of the Gates Foundation,[18] except that some of the greatest inequities are caused by the nature of our economic system and the inability of politics to change it. Global poverty, inequality, and violence can certainly be addressed, but doing so requires the empowerment of those closest to the problems, as well as the transformation of the systems, structures, values, and relationships that prevent most of the world's population from participating equally in the fruits of global progress. The long-term gains from changes like these will be much greater than those that flow from improvements in the delivery of better goods and services, but only the most visionary of philanthrocapitalists have much incentive to transform a system from which they have benefited hugely.

Business is certainly innovative in finding more efficient and profitable ways of doing the same kinds of things within the constraints and opportunities of the existing economic system, and these innovations will have some social impact, but business rarely innovates in the areas that lead to social transformation. They require a much more fundamental questioning and reimagining of how things are done. And the individual approach fails to recognize the power of collective action (whether organized through civil society or government), which can change the horizons of whole communities by implementing new laws and regulations, changing values and relationships, and cementing political coalitions and alliances from which everyone can benefit.

Indeed, when we look at examples of philanthropy that really make a difference, we see that they can't be measured at all by the yardsticks of business and the market. I'm thinking of groups like SCOPE (Strategic Concepts in Organizing and Policy Education) and Make the Road New York, both in the United States, which build grass-roots organizations, leadership, and alliances in communities that are most affected by social and economic injustice in Los Angeles and New York. Established after the Los Angeles riots in 1992, SCOPE addresses the "root causes of poverty" by nurturing new "social movements and winning systemic change from the bottom up."[19] It has involved almost one hundred thousand low-income residents in community action to secure a $10 million workforce development program with the DreamWorks Entertainment Corporation; developed a regional health care program funded by local government; initiated the Los Angeles Metropolitan Alliance to link low-income neighborhoods together in order to influence regional solutions; and launched the California State Alliance, which links twenty similar groups throughout the state to develop new ideas on environmental policy, government responsibility, and reforms in taxation and public spending.

Make the Road New York opened its doors in 1997 in the Bushwick section of Brooklyn to build the skills and strength of immigrant welfare recipients, but soon expanded its focus to combat the systemic economic and political marginalization of residents throughout New York. Since then, it has collected over $1.3 million in unpaid wages and benefits for low-income families through legal advocacy and secured public funding for a student success center to meet the needs of immigrants.[20] Both organizations are part of the Pushback Network, a national collaboration of community groups in six states that is developing a coordinated strategy to change policy and power relations in favor of those they serve from the grass roots up.

Outside the United States there are lots of similar examples. Take SPARC (the Society for Promotion of Area Resource Centres) in Mumbai, India, which has been working with slumdwellers since 1984 to build their capacity to fight for their rights and negotiate successfully with local government and banks.[21] SPARC—whose motto is "Breaking rules, changing norms, and creating innovation"—sees inequality as a "political condition," the result of a "deep asymmetry of power between different classes," not simply "a resource gap." SPARC has secured large-scale improvements in living conditions (including over fifty-five hundred new houses, security of tenure for many more squatters, and a "zero-open defecation campaign"); but just as important, it has helped community groups to forge strong links with millions of slumdwellers elsewhere in India and across the world through Shack/Slum Dwellers International (SDI), a global movement that has secured a place for the urban poor at the negotiating table when policies on housing are being developed by the World Bank and other powerful donors.

Housing is just a concrete expression of a much deeper set of changes that are captured in the following quotation from Arif Hasan, who works with SDI from his base in Karachi, Pakistan. "Traveling in different parts of the city as I did," he wrote after the unrest that followed Benazir Bhutto's assassination in December 2007, "you see nothing but burnt-out cars, trucks and trailers, attacked universities and schools, destroyed factories and government buildings and banks, petrol pumps and 'posh' outlets—all symbols of exploitation: institutions where the poor cannot afford to study; businesses where they cannot get jobs; government offices where they have to pay bribes and where they are insulted and abused. This is not a law and order situation, but an outpouring of grief and anger against corruption, injustice and hunger. . . . This is a structural problem that requires a structural solution."[22]

Groups like these do deliver tangible results such as jobs, health care, and houses, but more important, they change the social and political dynamics of places in ways that enable whole communities to share in the fruits of innovation and success. Key to these successes has been the determination to change power relations and the ownership of assets, and to put poor and other marginalized people firmly in the driver's seat—and that's no accident. Throughout history, "it has been the actions of those most affected by injustice that have transformed systems and institutions, as well as hearts and minds," as the Movement Strategy Center in California puts it.[23]

Symptoms vs. Causes

What do these stories have to tell us? First, that it is perfectly possible to use the market to extend access to useful goods and services. Second, that few of these efforts have any substantial, long-term, broad-based impact on social transformation. The reason is pretty obvious: Systemic change involves social movements, politics, and government, which these experiments generally ignore. One route alleviates the symptoms of some social problems more efficiently but leaves the deep structures of society pretty much intact; the other attacks the causes of social problems and tries to transform the systems that produced them. When you think about it, the latter is actually the most cost-effective route to social change, even if it takes longer and has many detours along the way.

Best of all are efforts like Shack/Slum Dwellers International and the others described above, which address both short- and long-term needs by linking together individual and collective action, service provision, asset building, advocacy, and empowerment. We "don't have to die in service to some abstract concept of social justice," as someone once put it to me when discussing philanthrocapitalist investments in getting drugs to people suffering from HIV; instead, we can address the production and distribution of these things in ways that also address social inequalities, build local economies, and strengthen the capacity of national health systems for the future. This is especially important where governments are weak and people lack access to essential services, as in much of the developing world, because immediate relief may be an essential precondition for their participation in long-term social action. But it is that long-term social and political action that matters most of all.

No great social cause was mobilized through the market in the twentieth century. In the United States, the civil rights movement, the women's movement, the environmental movement, the New Deal, and the Great Society were all pushed ahead by civil society and anchored in the power of government as a force for the public good. Business and markets play a vital role in taking these advances forward, but they are followers, not leaders, instruments in the orchestra, but not conductors. No lasting change has been successful without large numbers of people acting consciously and collectively around human values of solidarity and social justice, not market values. Markets are a great way to do some things, but not to fashion communities of caring and compassion.

Would philanthrocapitalism have helped to finance the civil rights movement in the United States? One hopes so, but it didn't fit any of the criteria that are at the top of the philanthrocapitalists' agenda: It wasn't data driven, it didn't operate through competition, it couldn't generate much revenue, and it didn't measure its impact in terms of the numbers of people who were served each day—yet it changed the world forever. Real social change happens by deepening this kind of broad, democratic movement and when disadvantaged groups gain enough power to effect structural changes in politics and economics.

Will societies be better placed to solve their problems when social activists are replaced by social entrepreneurs, when collective action is replaced by household asset building, when politics is replaced by technocracy, when mutuality is replaced by individualism, and when cooperation is replaced by competition? Such shifts are not inherently or always wrong, but they are certainly inappropriate as generalizations about social change and how best to support it, because business thinking and social transformation operate on entirely different logics.

To put it very simply, civil society and the market are asking different *questions*, not simply finding different *answers* to a question they hold in common about providing goods and services with more social impact. The failure to recognize this distinction undermines the long-term impact of market-based solutions to social and political problems. Is philanthrocapitalism a boundary-breaking movement or a symptom of a disordered and profoundly unequal world? It hasn't yet demonstrated that it provides the cure for global problems, that's for sure, but its proponents could argue that such judgments are severely premature. Nevertheless, changing the deep dynamics of poverty and dispossession is the test that all revolutionary ideas must pass.

CHAPTER TWO

The Good, the Bad, and the Ugly

When Business Thinking Advances Social Change—and When It Doesn't

All market activity has some social impact, just as all nonprofits and foundations—like the Ladies Auxiliary I mentioned in chapter 1—engage with the market in one way or another, though their links may well be very light. The real question is *what kind* of impact business can make on social change, and whether it preserves the status quo or brings about social transformation.

Businesses create jobs, ideally good ones with good benefits. Businesses produce and distribute goods and services, ideally ones that are socially and environmentally useful. And they stimulate technological innovation, ideally in areas that benefit the public good. The ways in which businesses approach these tasks have enormous implications for society at large, but in the past, the social and environmental impacts of core business decisions were seen as byproducts—not conscious goals—of companies, which aimed to make a decent profit and build shareholder value. During the 1990s, this assumption began to be questioned by the pioneers of corporate social responsibility, and their thinking laid the groundwork for the appearance of philanthrocapitalism ten years later.

By making their social and environmental objectives more explicit, so the theory goes, businesses can increase their positive impact and scale it up through market forces, far beyond the usual nonprofit project or government-funded program. And, arguing from the other side of the equation, by operating in the market and adopting business thinking, nonprofits can raise the revenue they need to expand and sustain their work and make it more effective. These ideas have given rise to a whole new vocabulary that tries to capture what is different about these interactions, including terms like *social entrepreneur*, *social enterprise*, *blended value*, *venture philanthropy*, *corporate social responsibility*, *the triple bottom line*, *social investment*, and *social innovation*.

There are no universally accepted definitions of any of these new terms. In fact, Pace University's Jeff Trexler, one of the most interesting commentators in this debate, thinks social entrepreneurship is "as open to interpretation as a Rorschach blot," taking whatever shape and meaning are in the eye of the beholder.[1] However, on one point the philanthrocapitalists are agreed: *Business* and *nonprofit* are crude labels that no longer describe the huge variety of activities that organizations undertake in circumstances where social and economic activities are increasingly intertwined, so it is not possible to criticize them en bloc for doing one thing or another.

In some ways this is obvious. Giant multinational companies usually behave differently from the mom-and-pop store down the street, just as a nonprofit hospital is not a community-organizing group or a broad-based social movement. Less obvious are the social costs and benefits of new experiments that go much further in blending civil society and the market in lots of different ways. Some use business thinking to manage nonprofit organizations and raise commercial revenue, and others deploy the techniques of venture capital investing in decisions about philanthropy. Some use the market to provide useful goods and services to lower-income and other disadvantaged groups, and others invest in new business models like *commons-based production* (in which innovations are collectively owned and goods are collectively produced). And there are many, many more of these experiments.

It's because of this huge variety of terms, approaches, and experiments that we need some basic clarity on what philanthrocapitalism *is*—not to enforce a single definition (that would be impossible) but to investigate the social impacts of different schools of thought. Otherwise, it won't be possible to know which blends are positive or to identify where business can help social change—and where it can't. The starting point for this conversation is to clarify the different ways in which business and the market are being used to advance social goals.

Pearls on a Necklace

In that sense, think of these experiments as pearls strung out along a necklace, each one representing a different mix of market and nonmarket values and activities. At one end of the necklace, one would find pure civil society activity, or as pure as is possible in a world where everyone must make a living and raise funds for the work they want to do. At the other extreme would be pure commercial activity, or as pure as possible given that business and the market should operate under rules and regulations that govern public safety and the like. And in the middle, one would find the philanthrocapitalists, not as a solid bloc but as a loose and diverse coalition of different approaches and motivations—radical, reformist, and all shades in between.

Within this broad coalition, *social entrepreneurs* are people "who work in an entrepreneurial manner, but for public or social benefit, rather than to make money."[2] They are "transformative forces who will not take 'no' for an answer" in their efforts to solve large-scale social problems. In his book *How to Change the World: Social Entrepreneurs and the Power of New Ideas*, David Bornstein includes Florence Nightingale, Mahatma Gandhi, Martin Luther King, and even St. Francis of Assisi, as well as people who have become standard-bearers for this new movement, such as Mohammad Yunus of the Grameen Bank and Bill Drayton of Ashoka.[3] What St. Francis would have thought about this designation is another matter, though someone who made a virtue out of humility hardly seems like a natural candidate. Still, Bornstein lists "a willingness to self-correct, break free of established structures, work quietly and develop strong ethical imperatives" as characteristics of successful social entrepreneurs, and the Italian certainly had all those in abundance.

Social enterprises are profit-making businesses established to tackle a social or environmental need. They are not new—nineteenth-century capitalism included space for many enterprises that existed for social as well as business goals, such as cooperatives, community banks, and credit unions—but the modern movement aims to be more influential in the mainstream by producing more and more goods and services through social enterprise, including Hollywood films with a social or environmental message (from companies like Jeff Skoll's Participant Productions), restaurants and food services (like La Mujer Obrera in El Paso), computer software (from companies like Benetech in California), and others that are cited in chapter 3. Social enterprises generate all or most of their income from commercial revenue, user fees, service contracts, and equity investments (rather than foundation grants, member dues, or individual donations), but they do not accrue profit for the personal gain of their staff or shareholders. They usually engage directly in the production and sale of goods and services, especially in areas like health, education, social welfare, environmental sustainability, and employment training. And they govern themselves through more inclusive and democratic practices than in a normal business, with avenues for participation by all their stakeholders. The essence of this movement is *blended value*, a process first described by Jed Emerson that creates hybrid institutions by combining elements from two different worlds—the *social* (meaning beyond the market or the individual), and the *enterprise* (meaning from business and the market).[4]

Venture philanthropists use business thinking to advance the social mission of foundations and other forms of giving. The hallmarks of venture philanthropy are "an entrepreneurial results-oriented framework, leverage, personal engagement, and impatience."[5] As befits an approach that emerged from the world of venture capital and Silicon Valley start-ups, "engagement" means direct intervention in, and a high measure of control over, the activities of the organizations that each foundation supports; effectiveness is measured using business metrics to monitor performance; strategy is dominated by aggressive revenue-generation efforts to promote financial sustainability and rapid "scaling up"; and "leverage" comes from pulling in resources from government and others and investing in a wider range of vehicles to achieve social goals—such as pre-purchasing new vaccines in order to lower prices while maintaining the profit margins that are required to cover the costs of R&D. "We can play on the entire keyboard," says Larry Brilliant, Google.org's CEO until his departure to the Skoll Foundation at the end of 2008.[6] It is interesting to note that the term *venture philanthropy* was first used by John D. Rockefeller III in 1969, and defined as "the adventurous funding of unpopular causes."[7] Whether present-day venture philanthropy lives up to this vision is an open question, but I'll admit that it has certainly enlivened the field, and that is a very good thing. As Peter Frumkin has concluded, however, "What seemed so new about venture philanthropy may have been the sizzle, not the content."[8]

Corporate social responsibility (CSR) covers a wide variety of activities that connect business to social and environmental goals through their supply chains, policies, and operations. At one end of the spectrum, CSR consists of corporate philanthropy and volunteering, and at the other end are activities that increase the social and environmental impact of the business while still sustaining profits—the *triple bottom line*.[9] These activities include certification and labeling schemes that set higher standards for sourcing and production; CSR monitoring schemes and metrics to which companies agree to hold themselves accountable; the global fair-trade movement, which has become especially strong in coffee, chocolate, diamonds, and other of life's essentials; and *community benefit agreements* that make superstores like Walmart reduce the damage they can cause. The most radical versions of CSR—called *third-generation* or *total* corporate social responsibility—go even further in assessing and addressing "how a company affects the societal systems in which it exists through *all* of its activities, including advertising and lobbying."[10] Although it's practiced by almost no one, that's a very powerful idea.

New business models take these ideas one step further. They attempt to change the ways in which companies operate at the most fundamental level by altering the legal structure of corporate governance, and producing goods and services through collaboration, not competition. Andrew Kassoy and his colleagues at B Corporation, for example, have developed a system that mandates companies to deliver benefits to all their stakeholders, not just to their shareholders.[11] Open source software and other forms of *nonmarket peer production* are already being used to create public assets like Wikipedia, showing how new business models can be built around *the commons*—the wealth we inherit or create together. Other examples include community-based economics and worker-owned firms that increase citizen control over the production and distribution of the economic surplus that businesses create; cooperatives like Mondragon, which has over one hundred thousand staff members in several dozen countries and has doubled in size every decade for the last thirty years; and different ways of sharing resources, such as *ecosystem trusts* and mutual funds that pay dividends to everyone, ideas that have been developed by Peter Barnes, the cofounder of telephone service provider Working Assets.[12]

Social investing supports all of these other innovations by directing more resources from financial markets to social enterprises, new business models, and companies that practice corporate social responsibility. Increasing numbers of individual investors are using their financial muscle in this way, but advocates of social investing are also trying to persuade large institutional investors such as pension funds and foundations to apply social and environmental criteria to their decisions, something that one might assume foundations already do. That's true for some but not for others, including leading philanthrocapitalists like the Gates Foundation, which found itself in hot water on just these grounds in 2008 when media reports criticized its reluctance to use its vast endowment as a tool for socially responsible investing.[13] There are even hopes that *social stock exchanges* might be established to bring innovations and investors together on a more formal basis, though some feel this is a distraction from "socializing" the stock exchanges we already have. In fact, some countries already have them, such as South Africa with SASIX and Brazil with its Social and Environmental Stock Exchange.[14]

Social innovation includes all of these other things under the broadest umbrella of all, defined as the process of finding innovative and effective solutions to social and environmental problems. Clearly, not all social innovations originate from business and the market, since they can and do spring from government and civil society too (think of the New Deal, for example, or social movements for civil and women's rights); but, at least among philanthrocapitalists, the link with business and the market is often assumed. And some important and effective routes to solving social problems are not especially innovative—they are approaches, such as advocacy and community organizing, that are proven but underresourced, and it always seems much easier to ignore them and focus on something new. Innovation may promote greater efficiency in how we use resources, but not greater effectiveness in how they are directed at the most difficult and complicated problems. And social innovation may not lead to social *transformation* at all.

Social transformation means much more than efficiency, effectiveness, and even innovation. The essence of transformation— like a butterfly emerging from a chrysalis—is a sense that something radically better and different can emerge from old patterns and structures when they are broken, shaken up, and superseded. In the social world, that means the patterns and structures that promote discrimination, dispossession and inequality, exclusion, violence, and the abuse of human rights. Power and empowerment are central to this process, because power lies at the root of anyone's ability to break with the status quo and invent new solutions. That is why confronting the powerful, and the power relations that shape society so deeply, is vital for social change. But to be truly transformational, these new solutions must also change the ways in which power is used—moving from domination to liberation—so that politics is more than a game of revolving chairs between narrow political factions, and economics is more than a process of individual advancement in which some get more of the pie than others. The British social commentator J. R. Bellerby put this well almost eighty years ago in his book *The Contributive Society*, when he wrote that the "ultimate test of any economic system must be the type of individual it tends to reproduce"—generous or selfish, peaceful or violent, competitive, cooperative, or somewhere in between.[15] And that's the test that should be applied to the philanthrocapitalist revolution.

Where Does This Leave Civil Society and the Nonprofit Sector?

I have been studying the world of voluntary citizen action for more than twenty-five years, and I still haven't found a definition of *civil society* that everyone agrees with. Some people include business and the market in their understanding of civil society, though that makes no sense to me since it mixes apples, oranges, and pears. Oxfam and General Motors are both *nongovernmental* organizations , but it is difficult to see why they should be grouped together when their functions and philosophies are so far apart. My interpretation is different and very simple: *Civil society* refers to the things we do together, not because we want to make a profit or earn a material reward, but because we care enough about something to take collective action. In every society, this kind of voluntary citizen action is expressed through a wide variety of forms, including community groups, advocacy organizations, labor unions, nonprofits, professional associations, religious groups, and social movements.

For civil society to operate successfully, there has to be a dense and dynamic ecosystem of these groups through which everyone's views and interests can be fairly represented. Manipulating this ecosystem through outside pressure or resources is always replete with risks, because it upsets the organic ways in which citizens shape their relationships with one another. These organic relationships make civil society complicated and messy, but also dynamic, fluid, and diverse. And that's something to be celebrated, even though I'm sure it drives some philanthrocapitalists absolutely nuts.

Although the lion's share of attention often goes to large nonprofit groups, they represent but a small proportion of total citizen action, and often not the most important. Over 73 percent of America's 1.4 million registered nonprofits have budgets smaller than $500,000 a year, and that figure excludes all the less formal groups that don't even have nonprofit status.[16] The reality of civil society is like an iceberg, with large and formal organizations as the peaks above the waterline and the great mass of citizen action underneath—less visible, maybe, but crucial in holding communities together and undertaking the collective work of a democracy. The real work of civil society, it could be argued, takes place down here, where the majority of America's 84 million volunteers are active.[17]

Why is civil society important? Not because it does one thing or represents one single point of view, but because it provides a space free of government control and the pressures of the market, a space in which private citizens can organize for *public* work—like protecting the environment, caring for each other, and shaping an ever-changing sense of the public or common interest. It's that independence that enables civil society groups to hold government and business accountable for their actions, and to act as crucibles for new or unpopular ideas, for democratic politics and the birth of social movements, and for speaking truth to power, whatever form that takes. These are spaces in which people learn the skills of equal engagement and negotiation with each other; nurture values of tolerance, cooperation, and compassion; and address problems that will never be solved through the market because there's no money to be made.

By itself, of course, civil society does not *bring* social transformation, since solutions to problems like poverty and conflict require government and business to put them into practice. But civil society is the place where these problems usually surface for attention, and from where pressure is exerted to make these institutions take up the challenge and perform in the public interest.

Therefore, nonprofits form only one part of civil society, and although many deliver services to those in need, civil society cannot be reduced to the role of a service provider in areas that are unprofitable for business. That is far too restrictive, and it misses the essential point about civil society's social and political importance. Public charities in the United States already receive over 70 percent of their income from fees for goods and services, so it is difficult to see why so much fuss is made about the newness of social enterprise.[18]

It's the same for the philanthropy that fuels civil society's activities, most of which has little or nothing to do with the institutional philanthropy of foundations and the big gifts of the superrich that usually take the headlines. Most philanthropy comes from small community and family foundations, which are growing rapidly across the world, and from individuals: Around 70 percent of U.S. households give money to civil society every year, some $307 billion in 2008.[19] Compare that with Google.org's projected spending of $175 million over the next three years, or the $100 billion that the Gates Foundation is likely to give away during the lifetimes of its founders;[20] it's a very impressive number to be sure, but a fraction of what could be channeled to social transformation by individuals (up to $55 *trillion* between 1998 and 2055 in the United States alone) and governments—at least $500 *gazillion* in the same period of time (OK, I made that one up).[21]

These observations are important, because money has a steering effect on those who receive it, and those steering effects will be different depending on the criteria and conditions that donors decide to impose. That's why the debate over venture philanthropy and other manifestations of philanthrocapitalism is so important.

The Good, the Bad, and the Ugly

It is clear from this brief tour of experiments and innovations that philanthrocapitalism includes lots of different approaches. Some of these approaches try to strengthen the social impact of economic activity, and others aim to build the economic sustainability of social action. Some do both, or at least claim to do so, but which ones achieve the best results, and which are window dressing? Do some actually harm the prospects of social change and social transformation, and have any achieved a scale that really makes a difference? Who belongs in the good, the bad, and the ugly?

THE GOOD

In separating the good from the not-so-good in these experiments, the key question is whether all the factors that influence social change are targeted for action, or whether business and

the market are the only tools employed. Many social entrepreneurs, for example, emphasize general attitudes of mind, defining *entrepreneurial* as energetic or single-minded in the pursuit
of a goal, and *businesslike* as professional and organized in one's
approach to one's work. Obviously, these attitudes are not the
property of the business sector, because they can be found in
government and civil society too, and they seem to have gone
missing from the companies that precipitated the financial crisis in 2008. In fact, they describe the characteristics of all effective organizations.

Others add a more explicit market twist to this definition.
"Social entrepreneurs typically pursue blended value returns
that may embrace the subjugation of a certain amount of financial return or take on added risk in pursuit of social and/or environmental value creation," says Jed Emerson.[22] In other words,
they accept less profit to do more good. Yet elsewhere in the
same movement, there are those who want to transform economic power structures and ways of living together, rather than
just using markets as instruments to deliver social goods—"not a
current *within* advanced capitalism but a challenge *to* it," in the
words of Rowena Young, the former director of the Skoll Centre for Social Entrepreneurship at Oxford University.[23] Those
who follow this interpretation put a lot more emphasis on supporting collective action and the empowerment of those usually classified as *beneficiaries* in order to seek systemic change in
public health, in education, and elsewhere.

These differences reveal an important tension between lion-
izing charismatic individuals—"pattern-changing social entrepreneurs as the most critical single factor in catalyzing . . .
transformation," to use Bill Drayton's words—and developing broad-based capacities for social and political engagement
that might make "everyone a change-maker" and force through

structural or systemic change.[24] "Faced with evidence of state incapacity to resolve pressing social problems," says Albert Cho, an academic who studies this field worldwide, "the social entrepreneur asks, 'How can I mobilize resources to solve this issue,' rather than 'Why does this issue exist?' When problems derive from politics rather than market failures, social entrepreneurs may well end up addressing symptoms rather than root causes."[25]

The same tensions run through social enterprise, which at its best goes beyond a concern to distribute the profits it makes in socially useful ways, to a larger commitment to produce those profits with more benefits and fewer costs—by paying higher wages, for example, and sourcing produce locally. Yet elsewhere in this movement, much more attention is paid to the *enterprise* side of this equation (and to the role of individuals as agents of social change) than to the *social*, beyond a limited vision of directing goods and services to lower-income groups or to groups that are marginalized for social and cultural reasons, such as people with physical or mental disabilities. Much of the literature on social enterprise seems to assume that the social will take care of itself if the enterprise is successful. *Social* usually signifies a target group, not a method of collective action, and that distinction is extremely important in terms of social transformation.

Even venture philanthropy is responding to these concerns. Although it is often left unsaid in the polite salons of the foundation world, the subtext of venture philanthropy is widespread dissatisfaction with the methods and achievements of older foundations, which are seen as analog players in a digital world. According to journalist Joshua Weisberg, "Just as Microsoft wanted to avoid becoming IBM, the Gates Foundation—despite protests to the contrary—dreads turning into the Ford Foundation."[26] But this, I think, is changing.

Having worked for an "old" foundation for the last nine

years, I am under no illusion about the fundamental changes
that philanthropy requires. Timidity, lack of focus, poor learning, weak accountability, and high transaction costs are all real
problems. But I doubt whether business and the market have all
the answers to the questions we face, or even whether venture
philanthropy is as innovative or effective as is claimed. "There's
nothing unusual about what we're doing," says Bill Gates Sr.
"We may have more money to spend, but that doesn't make us
different in kind, just in size." Melinda Gates adds, "We know
we didn't invent philanthropy or a new way of doing it. We have
relied so much on those who came before us."[27]

It's no coincidence that the old versus new, investor versus
bureaucrat, results versus process dichotomies of this debate are
already being eroded by foundations such as Omidyar, Gates,
and Skoll, which are moving slowly toward the kinds of investments in institution building, policy and advocacy capacities,
and governance that older foundations have pursued for decades
(with, it must be said, varying degrees of success). Gates, for
example, is investing millions of dollars in Shack/Slum Dwellers
International, one of the organizations highlighted in chapter 1.
The Skoll Foundation is helping an NGO called Peaceworks in
its efforts to connect Israelis and Palestinians who are commit-
ted to deepening the peace process within and across their societies. The Omidyar Network is investing heavily in civil society
development in West Africa through a new African foundation
called TrustAfrica. Richard Branson and others are supporting
interventions in conflict situations by the Elders, a group of emi-
nent statesmen and stateswomen whose numbers include Nelson
Mandela, Mary Robinson, and Jimmy Carter. And some of the
important commons-based experiments cited above are funded
by software companies such as Sun Microsystems and Microsoft, presumably not entirely without self-interest, given that
they rely on the infrastructure of computers and the Internet.

THE BAD

Less good, and merging into bad, is corporate social responsibility, or at least those parts of CSR that are closer to window-dressing than substantive reform—for example, Coca-Cola, releasing its first review of corporate responsibility at the same time as contaminating water supplies in India; Intel, which exited the One Laptop per Child project because of "philosophical differences" that turned out to be a more basic desire to protect its market for higher-priced hardware and more profits for itself; Walmart, now selling environmentally friendly light bulbs and the like but still engaged in "wage theft" (depressing living wages by withholding benefits and opposing unionization), as author Kim Bobo puts it; and a whole raft of oil companies, mining companies, supermarkets, and others whose performance in CSR doesn't match their public statements.[28]

As in these examples, too much CSR is a case of one step forward, two steps back, giving with one hand and taking with the other. After all, if business wants to save the world, there are plenty of opportunities to do so at the heart of their operations: pay your taxes as a good corporate citizen; don't produce goods that kill, exploit, or maim people; pay decent wages and provide benefits to your workers; don't subvert politics to pursue your short-term interests; obey the regulations that govern markets in the public interest; and stop creating monopolies and other market manipulations so that other firms can prosper and wealth can be more widely shared. As Daniel Landsburg put it on the Creative Capitalism blog, "If Archer Daniels Midland want to get creative, I'd like to see them abolish their lobbying arm and let the sugar quota expire." It's not exactly rocket science, is it? Yet some of the world's leading philanthrocapitalists have made their fortunes by creating vast monopolies in software and telecommunications before giving some of their

profits away to social causes. Carlos Slim, for example, controls
more than two hundred companies, accounting for 40 percent
of Mexico's main stock market index.[29] Does it make sense to
celebrate a system that skews the distribution of wealth so much
and gives so little back? Why not change the system itself so
that the rest of society can benefit directly?

An investigation by the U.S. Government Accountability
Office found that two-thirds of companies in the United States
paid no corporate income taxes in 2008.[30] Worldwide, developing countries lose $385 billion a year from corporate tax evasion,
far more than they receive in foreign aid, and leading philanthrocapitalists are not immune from this critique.[31] Google,
for example, paid only £600,000 in UK corporation tax despite
local revenues of more than $1.82 billion in 2007,[32] and avoid-
ed another $175 million in taxes to the Irish government in that
same year.[33] Mo Ibrahim, the billionaire philanthropist whose
foundation specializes in "good governance" in Africa, moved
from the UK to Monaco in order to pay less tax.[34] He is perfectly entitled to do that, of course, and there is nothing illegal
in any of these cases, but they give the worst possible example
to those who should be supplying much-needed tax revenue to
governments so that they become more accountable to their
citizens and have more chance of governing well. Unless the
philanthrocapitalists take up this central challenge and apply
CSR thinking consistently across their operations, the impact
of CSR on social transformation will continue to be slight.

AND THE UGLY

Are any of these activities downright ugly? No, not really.
There is still plenty of raw commercial activity in the global
marketplace that has no social or environmental screens at all,

especially in emerging economies where the pressure of price competition is so fierce and companies are trying to gain a foothold in the international system. However, this is capitalism, not philanthrocapitalism, so its shortfalls can't be used to attack those who do take their social conscience into work.

So Where Can Business Advance Social Change?

Like all religions, philanthrocapitalism inspires passionate adherence, opposition, and reflection from those it seeks to influence. It has its evangelicals who have drunk so much of the Kool-Aid that no amount of argument or evidence will shift their conviction that business is always best; its progressives who are actively seeking to transform society through revolutionary experiments in ownership, governance, and incentives right at the heart of business; and a broad center ground that is open to influence and persuasion from both of these directions.

From this quick tour of terms and definitions, it's obvious that each school of thought approaches the issue of social impact in a slightly different way. Pure commercial activity and corporate social responsibility of the window-dressing variety have little interest in deep social transformation. Pure civil society activity and most community organizers have little interest in becoming corporations. But in the middle, there are lots of ways of leveraging *some* social impact by working with the market in *some* shape or form.

In terms of their potential impact on social transformation, total corporate social responsibility, commons-based production, and radical interpretations of what it means to be a social entrepreneur are the most interesting approaches. They deliberately set out to use the power of the market to get goods and

services to large numbers of people, while simultaneously trying to alter patterns of ownership, consumption, production,
and accountability—they don't simply enable more people to
participate in the systems we already have. These experiments
recognize that far-reaching changes are necessary to transform
capitalism, rather than simply extending its social reach or ame-
liorating its social costs. And by *social*, they don't just mean a
part of society, such as disadvantaged groups who are identified
as targets for asset building among individuals. They mean the
full range of social structures, power relations, and strategies for
collective action and political mobilization that have historically
underpinned large-scale progress for exactly these groups. They
adopt some of the tools that business has to offer, but not the
underlying ideology of the market. And because the yin and yang
of social criteria and the market are coequal or head from civil
society to business and not the other way around, their impact
might go much deeper. In other words, the best experiments
use business thinking where it makes sense, and they use other
approaches where it does not. That may seem like a blindingly
obvious conclusion, but it is one that is easily lost in the hype
surrounding philanthrocapitalism. What does the evidence say
about these observations?

CHAPTER THREE

Missing Evidence

*The Change That Philanthrocapitalism
Doesn't Make*

Anyone looking for scientific proof that philanthro-capitalism does or does not work is sure to be disappointed. As chapter 2 made clear, different aspects of this movement are likely to have different costs and benefits; and although some serious studies of social enterprise and venture philanthropy exist, by and large the literature is anecdotal or written by evangelists more interested in publicity than rigor. This is not a field where self-criticism or humility will win you many plaudits. Nevertheless, there is some evidence to draw on, and plenty of experience against which to judge the claims that are being made in three main areas: extending access to useful goods and services among lower-income groups, strengthening nonprofit performance and the health of civil society, and improving national-level outcomes in terms of inequality and poverty.

The first claim is true but exaggerates the social impact of service provision and job creation. The second claim is untrue and disguises substantial damage to the world of voluntary citizen action. What distinguishes high-performing organizations is not whether they come from business or civil society, but whether they have a clear focus to their work, strong learning and accountability mechanisms that keep them heading in the right direction, and the ability to motivate their staff or volunteers to reach the highest collective levels of performance. And the third claim has never been true, even for the United States in the early phases of its development. Overall, there is no evidence that philanthrocapitalism achieves better results in solving social problems than traditional government and civil society activism.

Using the Market to Solve Global Poverty and Improve Public Health

Economists have always known that markets won't supply enough socially beneficial goods and services without subsidies and other kinds of help that provide incentives for the private sector to enter areas that are unprofitable, so the poor cannot get access to the loans, seeds, medicines, and other goods and services that they so desperately need. For many observers, providing these kinds of help is the natural territory of philanthrocapitalism, and the most exciting examples are the huge investments in global health, agriculture, and microcredit that the Gates Foundation is making, along with the Clinton Global Initiative and many other organizations. Given that someone dies from malaria every thirty seconds and that treated bed nets can be produced and distributed at very low cost, these investments are extremely important, and there is every reason to think that business and the market can help bring them to fruition. Even so, the latest guidelines from the World Health Organization recommend free distribution to ensure that they get to every-one who needs them.

The Gates Foundation is also investing in vaccines against the malaria parasite, along with similar efforts to defeat the scourge of HIV/AIDS, hookworm, leishmaniasis, and sleeping sickness. These efforts include encouragement for different lab-oratories to collaborate with each other, and at the same time spur innovation through competition—a nice example of rebal-ancing these different forces in a genuinely useful way—and a grant to the Public Library of Science to launch a new journal on neglected tropical diseases. The latter is the kind of investment that will help to build the public health capacities that are crucial for the future. Pharmaceutical companies are becoming enthusi-astic participants in ventures like these, including the Chicago-based Abbott Laboratories, which recently reached agreement with the Brazilian government to sell its popular HIV/AIDS drug Kaletra at a 30 percent discount. The same might be true for environmental goods and services in the future, since there is clearly money to be made from more-reliable solar-cooking stoves, energy-efficient light bulbs, and the like.

Efforts by the Gates and Rockefeller foundations to launch the new Alliance for a Green Revolution (AGRA) in Africa through genetically modified "wonder seeds" are more contro-versial, because of their high water and fertilizer requirements and impact on indigenous food systems, and because investments in land rights, roads, credit, and marketing have not been under-taken. Critics worry that companies like Monsanto that control large parts of the market for seeds and fertilizers stand to benefit unfairly, just as pharmaceutical firms will gain enormously from subsidies through the Advanced Market Commitment for new vaccines, another initiative with philanthrocapitalist involve-ment. Though AGRA "strengthens corporate opportunities

and power, it does nothing to address the weakened regula-
tory capacity of the state, the need to protect local markets or
ensure a fair market share of the value chain for farmers," says
African food activist Gala Gabirondo. "It elides [questions of]
land use and does not address the eroding economic and environmental resiliency of African food systems. Worse, it diverts
attention away from the role that global markets play in creating hunger and poverty in Africa in the first place. Can AGRA
solve these problems? Not without addressing their causes."[1]
Technical solutions to complex problems will always have their
limits, and these limits are beginning to show through in studies that evaluate the deeper social impact of this work.

For example, reports from the World Health Organization
and the Center for Global Development (an independent think
tank in Washington, D.C.) have revealed that large-scale investments in attacking TB, malaria, and AIDS were successful in
getting medicines to many of those who needed them, and in
setting up supply chains to safeguard these medicines during
storage and distribution. But because they focused so much on
the short-term problems of access and delivery, these investments weakened the national health *systems* that countries need
to treat problems effectively long into the future.[2] These studies covered World Bank and U.S. government funding as well
as funding from the Global Fund to Fight AIDS, Tuberculosis
and Malaria (which has received large donations from the Gates
Foundation, the Clinton Global Initiative, and others), so the
problem is not unique to the philanthrocapitalists. In fact, it has
been well known in the international development community
since the early 1980s, just consistently ignored or downgraded
by those who were looking for quick results. In addition, diar-
rhea, pneumonia, and intestinal parasites sicken and kill far more
people than the so-called big three of TB, malaria, and AIDS,
yet these problems have received far less investment.[3]

In similar fashion, a $258 million investment by the Gates Foundation in AIDS control in India has—according to its own evaluations—achieved none of the goals it set for itself and is too expensive to be handed over to the National AIDS Control Organization in New Delhi. Ten of the fifteen members of the management team came from business, including a CEO recruited from McKinsey and Company who had no experience in social change work and who embarked on a race to "franchise" programs to "consumers," including sex workers, many of whom were terrified when shiny new vans arrived at their brothels because they thought the vans were bringing the police. Communications took place in English, which few people understood, and people were paid to undertake activities for which they had previously volunteered, making it unlikely that they would volunteer again in the future. Expansion was too rapid and compromised the quality of what the program was trying to achieve.[4]

When donors become fixated on speed, scale, and numbers as indicators of success—just like in a business—it is easy to ignore the fact that new medicines are powerless when TB and malaria develop more resistance; or that the Green Revolution also increases inequality and workloads among farmers and their families; or that schools with rising enrollments lack teachers, desks, and textbooks. As Tanzanian educationalist Rakesh Rajani told the BBC, "Sometimes I feel we are just stuffing children into schools."[5] It doesn't help that immunization rates and other metrics are routinely overstated because the financial penalties of falling behind the curve are so great—assistance in this world being conditional on meeting time-bound goals and targets—but even if they were accurate at one point in time, they might not be sustained. The lesson is very clear: Don't sacrifice systems change for quick, material results. Invest in the capacity of countries and communities to manage and direct their own health care and other aspects of their development so that they can cope with whatever problems come their way.

MICROCREDIT AND THE "FORTUNE AT THE BOTTOM OF THE PYRAMID"

The other high-profile success story of philanthrocapitalism is microcredit or microfinance—in some people's minds, part of a broader claim that markets are the best way to eradicate global poverty. Although few rigorous evaluations of the impact of microfinance exist, it is clear that increasing poor people's access to savings, credit, and other financial services is a very good thing, and in one or two countries it has already reached significant scale—21 million clients and 105 million family members in Bangladesh alone.[6] Microfinance increases people's resilience, reduces their need to sell precious assets in times of trouble, and finances consumption, including spending on health and education that are vital for the future; but it doesn't move them out of poverty on its own. That requires other and more complicated measures to develop a sustainable livelihood and create more well-paying jobs through large-scale, labor-intensive agro-industrialization; to address the deeper issues of disempowerment that keep certain people poor—land rights, for example, or patriarchal social structures; and to get governments to redistribute resources on the necessary scale through health care, social welfare, public works, and education. There is some evidence that microfinance has a positive impact on the factors that lead to social transformation—women's empowerment, for example, and building small-group skills—but these advances have not translated into significant shifts in social and political dynamics, Bangladesh included.

Microfinance institutions also need continued subsidies from

government, philanthropy, or foreign aid in order to reach the
very poor, calling into question the philanthrocapitalist assumption that market methods, social goals, and financial sustainability are mutually supportive; and though their interest rates
are lower than those of local moneylenders, they are often very
high. When subsidies are abandoned, interest rates increase still
further, repayment is rigorously enforced, and the temptation
to become a conventional bank increases because of the potential profits that can be made—leading to accusations that microcredit groups have abandoned their mission to reach the very
poor in cases such as BancoSol in Bolivia and Compartamos in
Mexico. In April 2007, Compartamos, which started out as a
nonprofit provider of microfinance, sold 30 percent of its stock
for $458 million and turned itself into a private bank, bring-
ing enormous returns for its founders in the process (as well as
for the development agencies that had initially funded it), and
leading Alex Counts, president of the Washington, D.C.–based
Grameen Foundation, to conclude that the bank's poor clients
"were generating the profits but were excluded from them."[7]

The popularity of microfinance has spurred the use of similar techniques to provide other goods and services, such as cell
phones, nutritionally enriched yogurt and other foods, and even
health insurance. "The mobile phone . . . may be the developing world's Industrial Revolution for creating prosperity," says
the Hudson Institute in New York.[8] Grameen Phone in Bangladesh has achieved phenomenal success in spreading cell phone
use among the poor through female micro-entrepreneurs. Cell
phones do have a potential economic impact (on productivity)
and social impact (on civil society mobilization, for example),
but as Grameen Phone's founder once told me, "It's really just
good business." Besides, a sharecropper with a cell phone is still
a sharecropper (though maybe not for long?).

Perhaps the boldest claims for market-based poverty

reduction come from C. K. Prahalad, whose famous *bottom of the pyramid* (BOP) theory has become a core text of philanthrocapitalism by promising profits, poverty eradication, and empowerment all in a seamless package. Prahalad claims that huge, untapped markets lie at the base of the global income distribution (or pyramid) that—when supplied with goods the poor can buy and sell—will lift the poor out of poverty and also transform their lives socially and politically.[9] But "the fortune and glory at the bottom of the pyramid are a mirage," says Aneel Karnani, of the University of Michigan. "The fallacy of the BOP proposition is exacerbated by its hubris."[10]

Karnani and others have produced detailed evidence to show that many of the case studies used in support of BOP involve consumers who are not poor at all, and that the products and services that are sold by micro-entrepreneurs have less market penetration and productivity-enhancing potential than is claimed, so they will fail to produce sustainable incomes. Other evidence comes from an evaluation of Project Shakti, a public-private partnership promoted by Hindustan Lever (HLL) in India, which integrates low-income women into the marketing chain of its producers, selling shampoo, detergent, and other household goods in tiny quantities that the poor can afford "to boost their incomes and their confidence." Unfortunately, there is "no evidence that the project empowers women or promotes community action," as opposed to making them "saleswomen for HLL," often at considerable cost to themselves, as there are cheaper brands available, returns on investment are therefore low, and the work is very hard.[11] The subprime mortgage crisis in the United States provides a useful reminder that luring poor people into markets in this way is a dangerous affair.

Rather than focusing on the poor only as consumers, why not see and work with them as producers, activists, and participants in shaping the conditions under which they are offered market opportunities? As Richard Holla and Lakshmi Menon put it, "Philanthrocapitalists may wish to see more wealth trickle down to the poor, but NGOs—if they truly wish to minister to the needs of the poor—must strive to change the shape of the pyramid itself."[12] That is a good summary of the debate, I think, which turns on whether increased individual participation in markets is sufficient to transform society. The answer is clearly no. Extending access to useful goods and services benefits poor people as both producers and consumers, and it is only possible to achieve large-scale progress in this way by utilizing the power of the market. But that is the beginning of the journey toward social transformation, not the end, and it leaves everything else virtually untouched.

Given the number of people who benefit from microcredit in Bangladesh, it's likely that these programs have contributed to reducing poverty by around 17 percent between 1990 and 2005, though remittances and the successful export industries were certainly involved as well.[13] But Bangladesh remains a socially and politically dysfunctional state. In fact, no society in history has transformed itself through the recipes provided by philanthrocapitalism, and those that *have* had some success in reducing poverty and disadvantage have done so through government direction and civil society activism that steer the market toward long-term strategic objectives—think South Korea, Botswana, Brazil, Chile, and Taiwan. "The strength of the poor lies not in their assets but in their numbers," as I was once told by David Ellerman, an adviser to Joseph Stiglitz when all three of us worked at the World Bank in Washington, D.C., "and that strength is activated through the democratic political process and through pro-poor associations." Creating markets is not synonymous with solving social problems.

SOCIAL ENTERPRISE AND SOCIAL ENTREPRENEURS

When one takes the analysis down a notch or two and looks for evidence from richer countries, the same patterns emerge: Access to jobs and incomes, and goods and services, can be expanded through the market, but their social impact is restricted. Increasing numbers of initiatives are successfully using market methods to distribute goods and services that can benefit society. Examples include Think.MTV.com, an online community that serves as a platform for youth activism; Jeff Skoll's Participant Productions, which finances profitable movies with a message; video games with more positive algorithms; free channels for civil society groups on YouTube and other Web sites; RealBenefits in Boston, which produces software that enables families to access government aid with less bureaucracy; Sun-Night Solar, which produces solar-powered flashlights and sells them at a discount; the One Laptop Per Child program, which manufactures cheap computers running on open source software with help from Google and others in Silicon Valley; low-cost, self-adjustable glasses invented by Josh Silver, a retired Oxford professor of physics; Benetech, which is developing software to allow front-line human rights workers to record abuses in a way that is both automatically encrypted for security purposes and sufficiently rigorous to hold up in legal proceedings; and PATH in Seattle, which is partnering with TEMPTIME and the World Health Organization to manufacture vaccine vial monitors that will tell health workers whether vaccines can be used.

Then there are social enterprises that work with particular target groups or sectors—brokerage firms like Altrushare Securities, which makes profits from the stock market but shares them with struggling communities because it is owned by two nonprofits; La Mujer Obrera in El Paso, Colors in New York,

and the Farmers Diner in Vermont, restaurants that are owned
by their workers and privilege local produce; Bud's Warehouse
in Denver, a career and life-skills training program for people
who are rebuilding lives from addiction, homelessness, or prison; and Housing Works in New York City, generating $2 mil-
lion annually for its work with homeless people from its used
book store café (but still relying on grants for $28 million of
its $30 million budget). Social enterprises like these are espe-
cially common in the food industry, employment training, and
workforce development for low-income and other marginalized
groups, and in environmental goods and services like recycling,
since this is where enough demand exists to generate a profit at
a price point affordable to the poor.

These are important innovations, but the evidence suggests
that they are much more difficult to operate successfully on a
significant scale than the philanthrocapitalists admit, and that
they usually experience some trade-offs between their social
and financial goals. I haven't read every evaluation that has ever
been produced, but I looked at over two hundred scholarly and
policy-oriented studies of experiments like these and found a
clear pattern to their results. For example, a survey of 25 joint
ventures in the United States showed that 22 "had significant
conflicts between mission and the demands of corporate stakeholders"; and the two examples that were most successful in
financial terms deviated most from their social mission: reducing time and resources spent on advocacy because it was more
expensive than providing standardized services, weeding out clients who were more difficult to serve and had a higher per capita
cost, and focusing on activities with the greatest revenue-gen-
erating potential rather than those with the greatest potential
social impact.[14] Three volumes of academic studies covering a
further 175 cases revealed much the same conclusions.[15]

Detailed case studies of social enterprises carried out in the United States, made by the Seedco Policy Center in 2007, came to much the same conclusions. They include Community Childcare Assistance, which closed in 2003 after failing to secure the contracts it needed to operate successfully. "When organizations are expected to meet for-profit goals while operating under non-profit rules," the study concluded, "the double bottom line can become an impossible double-bind. . . . The more social responsibilities a venture assumes, the more difficult it is to succeed in the marketplace," and vice versa.[16] It is obviously possible to alter the balance between profits and social impact in the ways that all social enterprises aim to do, but there is no magic formula that removes the trade-offs that are involved. A survey of social enterprises in two regions of Italy (Lombardia and Emilia-Romagna), for example, showed weak effects on "deep empowerment" but a strong impact on "consumer empowerment," defined as "personal autonomy."[17] This is what one would expect from market-based activity, which rarely affects people's *collective* capacity to overcome key barriers to social progress.

What can we learn from evidence like this? It would be foolish to generalize too much from a few hundred cases, but this is the evidence we have, and it shows how difficult it is to blend the social and financial bottom lines. Few of these experiments are truly self-sustaining, mission drift is common, and failure rates are high. There is often less room to maneuver between mission and the market than one might think, and there are always trade-offs to be made—and they can compromise the deeper impact of this work on social transformation. Even when successful, social enterprises make soft targets for a takeover by conventional investors once they grow to a certain scale and profitability—think Ben and Jerry's, the Body Shop, and the

And 1 shoe company, which had all its social programs canceled when it was taken over in 2005.

Social entrepreneurs fare somewhat better, and there are certainly examples that are trying to bring service delivery, capacity building, and policy advocacy together. Between "49 and 60 percent of Ashoka Fellows have changed national policy within five years of start-up," which is impressive if those changes are more than episodic, though in my experience no better than other civil society activists who don't claim this mantle.[18] Teach for America is another good example, having trained almost 5,000 teachers, who are then assumed to participate in a movement for educational improvement;[19] and Green Dot, launched by Steve Barr in Los Angeles and now spreading across the country, also claims impressive achievements in turning round inner-city schools.[20] Indeed, public schools in America have become a veritable battleground for pro- and anti-philanthrocapitalist approaches to reform, and the popularity of entrepreneurial solutions is increasing, despite criticisms that "the business model of reform—competition, merit pay, union-busting, and data-driven—might be a great system for programming computers but it's a terrible one for an inherently humanistic endeavor."[21] Entrepreneurial organizations are ambitious and sometimes aggressive in pursuit of results, and that can lead them to exaggerate their influence and depth of innovation. "There's no secret curriculum-and-instruction sauce at Green Dot at all," says Don Shalvey, the founder of a charter school in California, "they're just doing old-school schooling."[22]

At their best, social entrepreneurs take the *social* side of the equation seriously, moving beyond the numbers game to consider the deeper issues of power and collective action. Nevertheless, the pull of the market is always very strong. Take, for example, the National Center for Social Entrepreneurs in Minnesota, which helps nonprofit organizations to combine "the passion of a social mission with a more strategic approach to today's current marketplace." When the rubber hits the road, however, it is the market that dominates decision making: "The safest and best opportunities for nonprofits to achieve greater short-term financial stability" include "reducing costs (for example: cutting programs no longer needed or valued by the market) . . . improving upon existing programs that bring about earned income . . . and identifying new opportunities that . . . fill a specific void within today's current marketplace."[23] This hierarchy of priorities is the reality for many social enterprises and social entrepreneurs for the simple reason that financial returns are a central part of their identity, but often it is unspoken or disguised.

The other problem is scale: Social enterprises had earned revenue of only $500 million in the United States in 2005. In Britain, they created 475,000 jobs (and $30 billion in value), which is substantial, though small in relation to the size of the economy.[24] In societies like the UK, where government and social enterprise are already symbiotic, nonprofit service provision can enhance public services, but where government is weak, it will simply add more patches to a quilt already full of holes. Business investment in global "goods" such as the environment and health potentially fares much better, since the market can work its magic if sufficient demand exists, and there is unlikely to be inadequate demand for life-saving vaccines, drugs, and products that can combat global warming, as long as corporations can turn a profit at prices that remain in reach.

Strengthening Civil Society

One of the most exciting times for any workplace is the arrival of a new CEO, but the day Saul Sockmaker joined

Community Arts Exchange (CAE) in Los Angeles, it was positively electrifying. In a parking-lot ceremony under a clear sky, most of the 360 CAE staff joined community leaders and board members to applaud Sockmaker, who ran 20 miles from his boyhood home carrying his Day One Business Plan, which he had presented during his first interview at CAE. Sockmaker's hiring was one more step in what the *New York Times* has described as "the trend in the nonprofit sector to recruit successful business executives in the hope that their expertise would instill greater professionalism and financial acumen." Half of CAE's employees would be sacked within six months, but on Sockmaker's first day, everyone was genuinely thrilled.

CAE was a unique twenty-five-year-old visual arts, job training, economic research, and HIV/AIDS program with a charter school, a sailing camp for children with disabilities, and a large contract with Mammon Bank to train inner-ring suburban single grandparents to become bond traders. CAE had always been run by its MSW founder, Marion Sandfort, so insiders were curious to see how a business-savvy MBA in charge might change things—especially someone so young and gifted as Saul Sockmaker. Board Chair Kate Barnsdorf paid tribute to Sandfort's many accomplishments: "CAE will miss Marion's passion for the mission, but today's economy demands a leader with business savvy and innovative approaches to assure CAE's future." Sandfort in turn thanked the board for its support and reflected that she had "tried my best and just used common sense since I didn't have business training." At the management meeting on day three of Sockmaker's tenure, it was clear there was a new sheriff in town. "This enterprise has an incredible mission, but hope is neither a business plan nor a capital structure. . . . In the next ninety days, there will be some restructuring. But first we are going to do a thorough review of operations and finance. I know there are efficiencies to be gained."

Sockmaker had made a fortune by the time he was thirty-five, taking proceeds from selling his Internet start-up to strike it big-time in Miami condos. By 2007, he realized that he needed to return to California to apply his business expertise by "giving back" to the community, and CAE's board encouraged him to name his price. Under a new CFO (hired from the Coalition Provisional Authority in Iraq), he announced a "rapid conversion to a dynamic enterprise accounting format." Something big was going to happen. On the first day of the board retreat, there was the Big Presentation, the product of four months of exploration and analysis. Alas, after all the buildup, the talk was mere puffery—going to scale with 1,200 percent growth in two years and dividing CAE into three "impact centers" with unpronounceable acronyms. Yet the board members were so jazzed that it was exciting and inspiring. What was not possible was determining precisely which things would change. That became clear the following Monday, when five of the long-standing programs were eliminated. Two months later, Sockmaker abruptly announced that he was leaving to become director of the Center for Social Entrepreneurship at Stanford's Business School and train the next generation of social capitalists. A smaller but wiser CAE is now 30 percent of its former self. Community Arts Exchange has decided to head back to its roots. If you know of someone with solid nonprofit management experience, please encourage them to apply.[25]

In case you haven't guessed, this is a spoof, written by Phil Anthrop, which I have adapted from America's leading magazine for the nonprofit community, *Nonprofit Quarterly*, but the experience it describes is real enough and has been played out numerous times in nonprofits large and small. In 2008, Planned Parenthood of America, for example, drew fire for building new, more stylishly appointed health centers as part of an effort to attract more-affluent patients and increase its revenue, and altered its mission statement accordingly in classic business style. Its mission used to promote the right to "reproductive self-determination" regardless of a person's income, but now it says that the organization will "leverage strength through our affiliated structure to be the nation's most trusted provider of sexual and reproductive health care."[26] This switch from human *rights* to human *needs* supplied through the market is a familiar theme in philanthrocapitalism, but something must be working, since Planned Parenthood has generated $1 billion in revenue and a cash surplus of $115 million.

The same tensions have been played out in many other nonprofits in America and beyond. Both the YWCA and the YMCA (America's largest nonprofit in terms of its earned income), for example, increased their presence in upscale urban areas in order to grow commercial revenue but faced questions about their social mission, and the YWCA saddled itself with millions of dollars of debt in 2003.[27] The Nature Conservancy was investigated by the U.S. Congress after public complaints about land deals with business, which aimed to safeguard natural resources through a variety of public-private partnerships, swaps, and sales but ended up in one almighty muddle, with the Conservancy forgetting that its purpose was not practicing real estate but fighting to preserve the environment. In retrospect, "it was wrong to get so close to industry," a senior staffer told the

Washington Post. "These corporate executives are carnivorous. You bring them in and they just take over."[28] "I've watched the growth in the domestic youth field of various philanthrocapitalism schemes with dismay," the publisher of *Youth Today* told me, "so much overhead, so much white-collar welfare, so little to show for it."

The Girl Scouts of America is undergoing dramatic changes drawn up by McKinsey and Company to "increase efficiency and uniformity" by consolidating local chapters—but is in danger of "depleting the very system that has . . . created the local investment and national prominence that the Girl Scouts enjoy today."[29] Reducing costs is an important priority for every citizens' group, of course, but that's not the bottom line for the Girl Scouts or any other NGO. It's far more important to support local commitment and initiative and see what grows from there. In fact, that's how civil society develops over long periods of time. Something similar happened to Habitat for Humanity, which was sued by one of its affiliates in 2008 to protest a new agreement on standards that had been imposed by the international office, thus reversing the autonomy that had enabled local groups to experiment with different ways of doing things that were appropriate to their contexts.[30] And to the American Red Cross, when management consultants encouraged the organization to adopt more sophisticated corporate planning (and planning was sorely needed in this NGO for sure). One manager observed, "If I were the owner of a business as opposed to a steward of the area's blood supply, I would jettison two-thirds of my customers."[31] Let's hope that he did not.

Not all nonprofits are heading toward the market. For example, the Visiting Nurses Association increased its commercial activities in the 1980s under pressure from for-profit health providers but dissolved them in 2000 because they simply were not viable. A survey of human services organizations in Canada by a team of researchers using NUD*IST4 software (yes, academics do sometimes have a sense of humor) analyzed how their mission had shifted out of existing activities and into "community counseling" as a result of the financial benefits that were supposed to flow from contracts in this area, "the big cash cows of the twentieth century . . . making counseling centers tons of money," and how they had failed, leaving the nonprofits that had extended themselves in this direction to get back to what they were supposed to be doing in the first place—serving people who couldn't afford to be served through the market.[32] And, as a study of twelve thousand environmental NGOs by the Stanford Business School discovered, "pragmatic" organizations fail more often than the "pure" ones—meaning those that do not compromise their principles to attract more revenue or public profile. This is partly because their supporters prefer the organizations they fund to operate without the compromises that philanthrocapitalism implies. As a result, membership and fund-raising are growing in pure organizations and declining in pragmatic ones. "Social movements are most effective," the study concluded, "when they are purest, most radical, and most disorganized."[33]

If these studies are in any way representative, then blending nonprofit and for-profit thinking could do significant damage to civil society as the philanthrocapitalist revolution rolls on. Civil society works best when its ecosystems are healthy and diverse, yet we know from careful historical research that these ecosystems have been eroded and distorted in many countries over the last fifty years. Diversity is declining as norms of good practice converge around a certain vision of professionalism and as resources are concentrated on the same kinds of organizations, usually those that speak the language of the funders and

can deal with their demands for data and reports. In the United
States at least, there are already signs of a growing fund-raising
divide between large national groups and smaller local organizations, and between those working on advocacy and service
delivery (who can raise funds more easily) and those working
on community organizing, grassroots capacity building, and
the crucial task of linking citizens across different issues, identities, and interests so that they can form broad-based alliances for change.[34]

Distance is increasing between advocacy groups and the
constituencies on whose behalf they are supposed to work, and
accountability is being reoriented upward to donors and government regulators instead of downward to communities at
the grass-roots level. According to Harvard professor Theda
Skocpol, the result is "diminished democracy"—the slow death
of organizations like Parent Teacher Associations (PTAs), the
American Legion, and the AFL-CIO that were locally rooted
but nationally active before and after World War II.[35] It was
these associations that built bridges between communities across
America and with the federal government, creating enough
civic and political energy to push through legislation like the
G.I. Bill of 1944, which led to dramatic gains in access to education and other widely shared social benefits. Such a triumph
would be much more difficult today because "technocracy has
transformed mediating institutions which once served as civic
meeting grounds—like locally grounded schools, congregations,
unions, and nonprofits—into service delivery operations," says
Harry Boyte, the leader of the civic agency movement in the
USA.[36] As a result, the nonprofit sector may be "getting larger, but weaker," says Pablo Eisenberg, a staunch critic of what
he calls the "corporatization of nonprofit groups."[37] As any
biologist knows, reducing diversity and breaking the organic

connections that link different animals and plants together is the death knell for any natural ecosystem. The same is surely true for civil society. As a report from the W. K. Kellogg Foundation puts it succinctly, "The emphasis on sustainability, efficiency and market share has the potential to endanger the most basic value of the non-profit sector—the availability of 'free space' within society for people to invent solutions to social problems and serve the public good."[38]

Philanthrocapitalism is not directly responsible for all these trends—they are rooted in longer-term social and economic forces—but it certainly encourages and accelerates them. For example, the increasing control orientation of donors that is such a feature of philanthrocapitalism is reducing the autonomy and flexibility of civil society groups, who are forced to spend and report on each donation exactly as prescribed. Paying volunteers may dilute people's willingness to serve in their communities for free. Energy and resources may be diverted away from structural change and institution building, in favor of service provision and social enterprise, where the real money and excitement lie. Dependence on the market may weaken civil society's ability to hold business accountable for its actions. And as nonprofits professionalize and distance themselves from any real sense of membership, they may cease to be training grounds for democracy and conduits for popular pressure from the grass roots. Welcome to civil society lite, the natural consequence of commercializing voluntary citizen action.

Business leaders are often scornful of the strengths of citizens' groups, criticizing them as amateur and riddled with inefficiencies in contrast to corporations. I have always been confused by the way in which some philanthrocapitalists differentiate themselves because they are "results based" or "high performance," implying that everyone else is uninterested in outcomes.

Sure, there are mediocre citizens' groups, just as there are mediocre businesses and government departments, so "why import the practices of mediocrity into the social sectors?" as Jim Collins asks in his pamphlet on nonprofit management.[39] There is also a tendency to make a fetish out of certain kinds of innovation that privilege business thinking, rather than looking at the impact that civil society makes on *its* own terms. The bedrock of citizen action may be effective but not especially new—I am thinking of the day-to-day work of solidarity and caring that wins no plaudits but is incredibly important in holding societies together. As a civil society enthusiast, I tend to ask the opposite question—namely, how come citizens' groups achieve *so much* when they are poorly paid, under-resourced, and up against the toughest problems facing our societies? Philanthrocapitalists are supposed to take great risks, but the real risk takers in philanthropy are civil society activists who risk their lives and livelihoods in situations of conflict and the abuse of human rights.

There is, for sure, a need to attend to salaries and benefits in the nonprofit sector, and I think that would certainly encourage better performance. But the business mantra of paying managers corporate salaries at the top of organizations is not the way to go. As far as I can see, there is no evidence that nonprofit results are tied to large increases in the pay of CEOs, but there is evidence that paying corporate salaries reduces public trust and thereby acts as a disincentive to giving over time. Compensation for the chief executives of the biggest U.S. charities and foundations rose at more than twice the inflation rate in 2006, according to a recent survey. In 2008, the United Way of Central Carolinas increased its CEO's compensation to $1.2 million a year along with a sixfold increase in contributions to her retirement fund.[40] The revelation of these figures prompted a wave of criticism from irate supporters who presumably expected their hard-earned donations to benefit those at the receiving end of injustice and discrimination. The same point could be made about for-profit fund-raisers who may generate more money for the nonprofits that employ them, but who cream off overheads that would make any charity faint—up to ninety-four cents of every dollar in the case of those who worked, in a delicious irony, for Citizens Against Government Waste in California.[41] By contrast, the real returns would come from smaller increases in salaries and benefits across the broadest range possible of nonprofit workers. A properly funded pension scheme and health insurance for all community organizers would be among the best investments that could be made. Are there any philanthrocapitalists out there who will rise to that challenge?

The other weaknesses of nonprofits that are constantly pointed out lie in management and planning, weaknesses that are supposed to be corrected by the strong control and intervention of venture philanthropists and the burgeoning industry of intermediaries and management consultants they fund. It's interesting to note that incompetent companies and banks wanted help with no strings attached when they were bailed out by the U.S. government, but nonprofits are supposed to accept intervention by philanthrocapitalists with a large and grateful smile. Consultants can certainly shed fresh light on problems, shake up hierarchies, and identify necessary improvements in systems and in structures, but nonprofit managers have just as much to offer, because they can also see things in significantly different ways: mobilizing teams through less hierarchical and centralized structures, for example; using reflective and contemplative practices to improve their performance; developing accountability mechanisms that bring in all their stakeholders and measure impact in more creative ways; and being more flexible in dealing with conflicting views. In fact, a recent study by *Nonprofit*

Quarterly found that nonprofit leaders were more effective than their for-profit counterparts in fourteen out of seventeen dimensions of leadership practice, including risk taking, persuasiveness, and vision.[42]

There are no neutral ways of dealing with the management questions that all organizations face, because they imply making value judgments about what is important and effective in each particular context. It is easy to identify quick fixes in terms of business and market criteria, only to find out that what seemed inefficient turns out to be essential for civil society's social and political impact—as in the cases of the Girl Scouts and Habitat for Humanity described in brief above. The idea that investments in social action should be cost-effective is too often conflated with a particular (market) definition of efficiency, partly because groups like McKinsey and Company have so little direct and textured experience in the deeper dimensions of citizen action that were highlighted in chapter 1. A leading Indian social activist put it to me this way: "In a world falling apart with the financial crisis, the nonprofit sector is a good haven for management consultants. Lots of money to pontificate about obvious things, very little questioning of the fact that you can cover your ignorance of fields and issues through management jargon, no accountability to anyone for mistakes arising from your lack of experience or plain ignorance, and plenty of arrogance to boot." That's a harsh judgment, but it reflects a real sense of anger and suspicion in the nonprofit world that is rarely expressed in public because of fears of retribution.

None of this means that companies like McKinsey, Bridgespan, and others are irrelevant or always wrong. They are increasingly active in the nonprofit world, and the services they offer are often very useful. In his "Report from the Front Lines," Eric Schwarz, the founder of Citizen Schools Inc. (a U.S. social enterprise), accepts that the substance of what such companies bring has helped his organization considerably, but he rejects as "flawed and highly offensive" the implication that this proves private sector superiority.[43] I have used these companies myself to great effect, when nonprofits are trying to raise their own revenue and require a solid dose of business planning, market testing, and skills in financial forecasts. But most civil society organizations don't need these things to do their work effectively, because they have nothing to sell or trade, and for them there are many routes to financial sustainability that don't involve the market. Maybe these are better, since they might do less damage to their social mission.

Obviously, someone has to pay for any activity that incurs a cost, even if it is led by volunteers, but this doesn't necessarily imply the raising of commercial revenue. Philanthrocapitalists sometimes paint reliance on donations, grants, and membership contributions as a weakness for nonprofits, but it can be a source of strength because it connects them to their constituencies and the public—as long as their revenue streams are sufficiently diverse to weather the inevitable storms along the way. In many cases, this would be a safer bet than pulling in more revenue from commercial capital providers with all the risks that that entails—for example, from the Lehman Brothers Foundation or Bernard Madoff's "management" of investments by nonprofits.

"Nonprofits must understand that the desire to earn income and the desire to use business practices to promote social change are two different and almost entirely incompatible objectives. . . . Don't mix your models," warns the Seedco Policy Center in New York.[44] Introducing the different logics of civil society and the market into the same organization can have a negative effect by confusing the bottom line still further, complicating accountability and stimulating mission drift. Concentrating investment in a few large organizations, standardizing production and management information systems, and enforcing easily measurable indicators of short-term success—these are the lifeblood of a successful company but the death knell of a thriving civil society.

National Social and Economic Performance

Finally, we can look at the macro level—the level of national social and economic performance—to see what happens when markets replace public or pure civil society provision. Much has been claimed for market methods over the last few decades, and in some fields they have produced real gains, but experience with privatizing utilities and pensions has been at best uneven and at worst both inefficient and socially divisive. Infamous cases include the British consortium that ended up in prison after privatizing the water system of Dar es Salaam in Tanzania, and the notorious water wars in Chile and Bolivia that increased water prices in the latter by 43 percent, part of a raft of failings that helped push Latin America to the left after 2001. Worldwide research by the United Nations Research Institute for Social Development in Geneva shows that countries with longer life expectancy and lower under-five mortality spend a significantly greater proportion of their GDP on *government* health care, not private or social enterprise.[45] As Laurie Garrett has shown, the one thing necessary to address global health pandemics like HIV/AIDS is a strong public health infrastructure, not a patchwork quilt of private and social provision.[46] Sustained health progress requires that technological advances be integrated with the redistribution of political power and broadly based participation in the economy.

Both recent history and contemporary experience suggest that the best results in raising economic growth rates while simultaneously reducing poverty and inequality come when markets are subordinated to the public interest, as expressed through government and civil society. Public and private interests must be separated so that governments have the autonomy they need to oversee development. This was true in East Asia after 1945, when the so-called Asian tigers increased their GDP from a level comparable to that of Chad, Pakistan, and Haiti to a level that rivals that of parts of Western Europe; it was true in other successful experiences of international development such as Chile and Botswana in the 1980s and 1990s; and it is true of China and Vietnam today. Some would say it was even true of the United States in the nineteenth century. In all these countries, business was encouraged to do its thing, but in service to long-term goals that favored redistribution and social stability by "governing the market," in the words of a famous book by Robert Wade.[47]

Today, countries that practice similar policies score highly on their social indicators (think Sweden, the Netherlands, and Canada), while those, like the United States, that have strayed from this path remain more violent and unequal, although they can still enjoy high rates of productivity growth in their economies. The United States has become one of the western world's less socially mobile societies and has delivered stagnant incomes to a large minority over the last thirty years. Meanwhile, the share of national income accounted for by the top 1 percent of earners has reached its highest level since 1928, at almost 22 percent.[48] In terms of the latest global rankings of life expectancy, America has dropped from eleventh to forty-second place in the last two decades. Things look better on the Environmental Performance Index, composed each year by Yale (the United States is twenty-eighth), but now the *Economist* Intelligence Unit, working with Vision of Humanity, has devised a Global Peace Index that puts the U.S. so far down the ranks that even

Syria and Burkina Faso score higher (the reason is America's huge prison population, easy access to firearms, and burgeoning military budget).[49]

As a whole raft of authors have discovered, capitalism, at least in its present condition, has also produced a measurable decline in our emotional well-being, "crippling personal agency despite the avowals of individual choice"[50] and producing a range of "social poisons," including rising greed and envy, rampant fraud and dishonesty, falling trust, and a crisis of ethics in nearly every area of life.[51] Inequality has profound social consequences in all these areas and more, which is why more equal societies almost always do better.[52]

In each of these three areas—service provision, civil society effectiveness, and national-level outcomes—the evidence in support of philanthrocapitalism is not persuasive, and is still less so if one looks for results in terms of the transformation of society. "Social business," as described by Muhammad Yunus, the inspirational founder of the Grameen Bank, is much better than "antisocial business"—that's for sure—but as the experience of the industrialized world shows quite clearly, eradicating poverty and other social ills requires much more than an effective and accessible banking system, or adding micronutrients to our food, or manufacturing solar-rechargeable light bulbs and the like. Philanthrocapitalism will only ever be part of the solution to the problems we face, especially if our goal is to abolish all forms of violence, oppression, and discrimination. Redistributive politics, government intervention, social movements, civil society activism, vibrant public spaces, and deep personal change will continue to be crucial ingredients of any successful agenda for reform. Why does involving business and markets in social change produce such mixed results?

CHAPTER FOUR

The High Cost of Mission Drift

*Why Human Values and Market Values
Don't Mix*

A t first sight, the belief that capitalism will spread
equality and justice throughout the world seems
far-fetched. How can a philosophy rooted in money and self-
interest give rise to societies that are ruled by love? After all,
markets were designed to facilitate the exchange of goods and
services under a limited definition of efficiency that had little
to do with moral or social goals. Yet the broader effects of capitalism have animated debates in all societies at least since Adam
Smith, who was so agitated by this question that he wrote two
different books in search of a single answer. One of them changed
the world, and the other, sadly, has all but been forgotten.

The Wealth of Nations describes how economic forces will
produce the greatest common good under conditions of perfect
liberty and competition, maximizing the efficient allocation of
productive resources and bringing the economy into equilib-
rium—"the ideal balance between buyers and sellers, and firms
and workers, such that rates of return to a resource in various uses will be equal."[1] The "invisible hand" makes only one

appearance in the 1,264 pages of my edition (it's on page 572), perhaps because Smith didn't believe that social welfare would be maximized through the uncoordinated (i.e., "invisible") actions of self-interested individuals. It was later economists like Milton Friedman who claimed that the efficient operation of the market would always create more social value than would altering or redistributing the surplus it produced through philanthropy or government intervention. Smith did warn against the dangers of "social engineering," but he also celebrated the importance of nonmarket values, including "sympathy."

That is why *The Theory of Moral Sentiments* (Smith's earlier book, and the one he thought was more important) explores the personal behaviors required of individuals to control their wants and recognize the needs of others. "The wise and virtuous man," he wrote, "is at all times willing that his own private interest should be sacrificed to the public interest of his own particular order or society." Following our own self-interest to secure the basic necessities is only the first step toward the higher goal of achieving a virtuous life, attained by actualizing our capacity for what Smith called "benevolence." Yet he was unable to integrate these two books into one coherent philosophy, sparking a conversation between efficiency and welfare that continues still today. Will philanthrocapitalism finally resolve Adam Smith's dilemma?

In conventional market thinking, "the social responsibility of business is to increase its profits," as Milton Friedman famously declared almost forty years ago in the pages of the *New York Times*. That is because the invisible hand is supposed "to be beneficial for the people it orders," maximizing social welfare as a by-product of self-interested but unconscious interactions, with some light regulation to ensure that business operates inside a framework of agreed-upon social rules.[2] One of the virtues of markets is that, at least in theory, they can ensure that each resource is used where returns are highest and is combined with other resources in the most efficient way, even though producers and consumers do not coordinate their decisions. Philanthrocapitalism gives this theory an extra twist by adding more explicit social and environmental considerations into economic decision making, but the drivers of change are still *internal* and *relatively unplanned*—otherwise, efficiency would suffer because bureaucrats would second-guess what only markets can decide. To what extent, however, can markets change, correct, or transform *themselves*, or would that be like asking a man to pull himself out of a swamp by his own hair—just as markets were supposed to do prior to the financial crisis, when self-regulation obviously failed? This question goes to the heart of the debate between philanthrocapitalism and other, more traditional approaches to social transformation. One school of thought sees progress as the automatic result of the efficient workings of the market, and the other sees it as the outcome of conscious interventions in markets through politics and civil society activism.

In this second school of thought, social change is usually a deliberate goal to be achieved through collective action by civil society or government, though not necessarily using the kind of social engineering that worried Adam Smith. Civil society is also the outcome of interactions by millions of dispersed individuals and organizations, but all acting with some sense of social purpose. So the energy here is *external* and *explicitly directed* at leveraging some kind of broader social impact, including getting governments to tax and regulate the business sector so that it contributes more to the public good. "In the end," writes James Gustave Speth of Yale's School of Forestry and Environmental Studies, "a responsible company is one that is required to be responsible by law."[3] That's why the independence of government and civil society is so important. "The move to distinguish social enterprise from private enterprise suggests that social objectives *stand distinct* from the interplay of individual pursuits."[4]

Markets work well when they stick to a clear financial bottom line, use a single mechanism to achieve it (competition), and satisfy a simple set of conditions that make that mechanism work, such as the presence of multiple sellers from whom buyers can choose and access to information about them for consumers. Social change, by contrast, has many bottom lines and strategies to reach them, and it relies on forces that are outside the control of any one set of institutions. Economic efficiency is not the same as human fulfillment, and market norms do not properly express the valuations of a democratic society for all sorts of well-known reasons: They don't price real assets such as the environment and social cohesion, they can't represent the needs of the future in the present, and they are full of imperfections that lead to problems like monopoly. That is why we need alternative allocation mechanisms through government and civil society for things like public spaces or access to the Internet, which markets would distribute unequally, if at all.

The profit motive is not a dirty word, but it is a different word from solidarity and caring with no expectation of return. These differences cannot be wished away. They are rooted, often unconsciously, in different worldviews and cultures. But market values and human values are not just different; they pull in opposite directions in many important ways, and the risks involved in mixing them together are apparent in the evidence reviewed in chapter 3. Unless those risks are recognized, it won't be possible to identify when business thinking can help social change and when it can't.

Wants, Needs, and Rights

The raison d'être of markets is to satisfy personal wants according to the purchasing power of each consumer, so expecting "creative capitalism" to serve poorer people doesn't make much sense against the background of large-scale inequality. By contrast, civil society exists to meet needs and realize rights, regardless of people's ability to pay. There is no price of entry to civil society except the willingness to work together. Of course, people can still be excluded from participating in citizens' groups for social or political reasons, but rarely because of a lack of effective demand.

As a result, attitudes toward economic inequality vary greatly between these two worlds. Some claim that markets act as the great leveler in democratizing power (by honoring consumer choice). It is true that markets, capitalism, civil society, and democracy evolved in tandem, but democracy and civil society worked hard to contain and channel the enormous energies of capitalism and to contain its tendencies toward inequality. Again and again, they sought to assert the principles of equality and rights—to minimum wages or fair treatment for the disabled—just as civil society has repeatedly campaigned to make it harder for wealthy minorities to manipulate democratic institutions to their own advantage. Equality is the foundation of all healthy and democratic relationships, and the key to a civil society in which everyone can participate—philanthropy as everyone's business versus the business of philanthropy, bottom-up versus top-down, meaningful redistribution versus larger crumbs from the rich man's table. As Gary Cross has written, "A society that reduces everything to a market inevitably divides those who can buy from those who cannot, undermining any sense of collective responsibility and with it, democracy."[5]

The Mexican philanthrocapitalist Carlos Slim recently donated $50 million to purchase cheap laptop computers for children in Mexico and Central America, but would you rather rely on the generosity of the world's third-richest man or have the wherewithal to buy a computer for yourself as a result of fundamental changes in the economic system? "Wealth is like an orchard," Slim goes on. "You have to distribute the fruit, not the branch," presumably because most branches of the Mexican economy now belong to him.[6] In a column in the *Nation*, Daniel Brook describes the "social Darwinism" that returns as the "ideology of all gilded ages" to justify rising inequality. "The rich don't exploit the poor," Brook says. "They just outcompete them."[7]

Competition, Cooperation, and Collaboration

Philanthrocapitalism assumes that competition will make civil society more efficient and thereby bring more social change, but this is a particularly damaging form of social Darwinism that misreads the way social change actually occurs. Effective markets are characterized by healthy competition against a clear bottom line, obsessively pursued in the case of Walmart, for example, and its prices. Even companies that practice "triple bottom line" accounting revert to finance when hard decisions must be made, because businesses are legally structured to deliver shareholder returns. Civil society, by contrast, faces many bottom lines, and works through cooperation and sharing to achieve them. There is competition in civil society too, of course, for funding and allegiances, but it's not the basic mechanism through which citizen action works. That's because civil society is good for many things where competition would be illogical or ineffective, such as building the social fabric of a community. Social commitment, love, and solidarity—these qualities underpin performance just as powerfully as competition and the desire for market share.

"In the past," says David Bornstein, "citizen-sector organizations have been insulated from the forces of head-to-head competition. However, as the sector continues to attract talent, competition is likely to intensify, *particularly as social entrepreneurs seek to capture the benefits of their innovations* [my italics]."[8] This is an odd statement, implying that social innovations have to be "captured" for private benefit when they are supposed to benefit the public good. He goes on to claim that competition will promote collaboration because weak performers will copy strong ones, an assumption that ignores how citizen action actually works—collegially but in different ways for different purposes and constituencies. "Unproductive citizen-sector organizations can plod along ineffectually for decades," he says, but others might just as reasonably say that they work quietly creating results that his metrics do not and cannot count. Who is to say which interpretation is correct?

Competition might even make things worse, by pushing non-profits to economize in key areas of their work, eschewing the most complicated and expensive issues and avoiding those most difficult to reach. And outside of service provision, it is difficult to see how competition would make any sense at all, and not just because the relevant market conditions are unlikely to exist. Are women's rights competing with civil or political rights, or HIV prevention with public school reform? Would there be increasing competition between voluntary fire and ambulance brigades, or Moose and Elks, or groups dealing with different issues like homelessness and domestic violence? Would the Ladies Auxiliary compete with other groups to host the children's Christmas

party? And who would benefit from any of these things? Unlike
in markets (where I can buy from whomever I like without caus-
ing too much social damage), organizations in civil society are
not easily substitutable because affiliations are based on loyalty,
identity, and familiarity, not on the price and quality of services
provided. It's unlikely that members of the National Association
for the Advancement of Colored People (NAACP) will cross
over to the Puerto Rican Legal Defense and Education Fund if
they feel dissatisfied with their organization and its performance.

Si Kahn, one of America's leading social activists, once put it
to me this way: "There are twenty other organizations as good
as or better than us—it's not a competition. I'm a movement
person, and at a very deep level it doesn't matter whether we
get a grant or someone else does, so long as the movement has
enough money to do its work." Imagine a business saying that.
As an unnamed social activist said to researchers Carol Chetkovich and Frances Kunreuther, "We are steadily losing . . .
the really strong, absolute basic instinct that collaboration and
mutual support comes first. And to the extent that we lose that,
it really, really weakens the movement."[9] That's the thing about
competition—some people win, and many others lose.

Individualism, Solidarity, and Collective Action

Markets deal in contracts, from which I expect delivery at the
price that we agreed, whereas civil society deals in friends and
neighbors, from whom I expect support, come what may. "Don't
buy from friends" is wise advice, so don't expect solidarity from
business either. Market norms are impersonal, characterized
by the freedom to disconnect, to switch to a different suppli-
er whenever and wherever I may want. This isn't a convincing

basis for a healthy and successful society, which requires a commitment to each other and to the public good, and the loyalty to hang in there for the long haul of social transformation even when the going gets tough and things turn against you. There is no responsible exit from civil society and the duties we hold in common.

What lies at the core of markets is individualism and the role of the entrepreneur as the prime mover of growth and change. What lies at the heart of civil society is collective action and mutuality, which challenge the increasing atomization of society. Yet Jeff Skoll is proud to say that social enterprise "is a movement *from* institutions *to* individuals," because they "can move faster and take more chances."[10] Indeed they can, but can they also generate system-wide changes in social and political structures that rely on collective action and broad-based constituencies for change? In his pamphlet *Everyone a Changemaker*, Bill Drayton describes how social entrepreneurs "decide that the world must change in some important way . . . and build highways that lead inexorably to that result,"[11] but social transformation requires broad-based participation and democratic accountability—negotiated solutions, not blueprints forced through from the top. Wherever systemic change has already been achieved—for example, in relation to the environment, civil rights, gender, and disability—it came about through the work of movements rather than heroic individuals, even though leadership was obviously important. For every successful leader there are hundreds of unsung heroes and heroines who stand behind success.

In markets, we are customers, clients, or consumers, whereas in civil society we are citizens, a designation that carries a different set of responsibilities and rights. Markets process and deliver, whereas citizens' groups engage in co-creation, shared responsibilities, and the mobilization of people around a common cause. In fact, social movements do worst when they internalize the logic of the market, fracturing into pieces that attempt to defend their particular territory and approach. Processes in civil society revolve around participation, which is far too messy and time-consuming for business to embrace. In fact, the voices of low-income and other marginalized people are almost completely absent from the literature on venture philanthropy and social enterprise, where things seem to be done to, for, or around but never with or by them. Will the poor be written out of their own story once again? Social transformation involves changing *our* values and relationships, especially with those who have less power, and the only way to do that is by being present with people and allowing them to hold *you* accountable for your actions. "Power always thinks it has a great soul and vast views beyond the comprehension of the weak," said John Quincy Adams, the sixth president of the United States. But this is almost never true, leading to a long history of failed projects that have ignored the voices of those they were supposed to help.

Current trends in fund-raising may contribute to this problem, reducing the transaction costs of donating to good causes but failing to engage givers and receivers in any authentic collaboration outside of writing a check or clicking a mouse on Web sites like Kiva and GlobalGiving. A huge amount of publicity, and a small amount of additional money, has been generated by Kiva and the like, and that is always welcome, but they deemphasize community involvement and skew accountability to those who already have more power, so what are they actually transforming? Or take Microsoft's IMproved, which shares a portion of its advertising revenue from Hotmail with charities that users can select. "It's an incredibly easy way to address the issues you feel passionate about, including poverty and environmental degradation," as the publicity machine declares, much easier than rolling up your sleeves and actually getting involved in action on challenges like these. Sidney Verba, who has studied civil society in the United States throughout the last forty years, calls low-engagement fund-raising the "junk food" of participation—satisfying to the stomach but unhealthy for building strong communities over long periods of time.

Technocracy, Politics, and Protest

In the ever-growing outpouring of books, newspaper stories, and conference reports on philanthrocapitalism, you will find plenty of attention to finance and the market, but scarcely a mention of power, politics, and social relations—the things that drive social transformation. One approach helps individuals to enter the market and move up through the existing hierarchies of society, and the other tries to demolish those hierarchies so that they can be replaced by something new. Although the landscape is shifting a little as experience develops, the majority of venture philanthropy supports technical solutions and rapid scaling up: Technology plus science plus the market brings results. "The new philanthropists believe there must be a magic bullet for everything, an instant cure for poverty," says Sanjay Sinha, managing director of Micro-Credit Ratings International Ltd. in India. "They are not willing to believe that poverty reduction is a far more complicated matter than the idea of eBay."[12] Billionaires have little experience of *not* having power (except maybe prior to their success), of *not* being in control, and of *not* being able to predict what is going to happen to prices, sales, and profits.

Two contrasting views from India encapsulate this debate. "Philanthrocapitalism is structurally incapable of addressing social justice. To expect them to fund their own loss of power is almost tragic-comic," wrote an exasperated Indian fund-raiser in a private e-mail to me. On the other hand, Rohini Nilekani wrote the following in an op-ed piece in the *Hindu* in July 2008; Nilekani herself is a philanthrocapitalist as chairperson of Arghyam, a foundation endowed with profits from the software company Infosys: "A lot of us, especially in the newer foundations, are in a big hurry to achieve social change. Yet there are some things we must ask ourselves honestly. Do we want to address the symptoms of social inequity, or do we want genuine social transformation? If so, who are the real agents of such a transformation? And to become change agents ourselves, what are the values we must embrace?"[13] Underwriting the distribution of retroviral drugs is obviously important for those with HIV, but what about reforming the patent protections that make them so expensive? Should Microsoft be praised for training teachers in the use of their computers, or criticized for offering free or subsidized proprietary software when Indian states like Kerala are promoting open source software in their schools?

Where philanthrocapitalists see the need to correct the "market failures" and lack of economic incentives that lie at the root of the problem, civil society names and attacks the realities of injustice, such as racism, sexism, homophobia, and the abuse of human rights—terms that rarely appear in the strategic plans of any of the new foundations. I don't think this is just semantics. Their own lobbying discounted, it comes from businesses' aversion to the kind of protest and hard-edged advocacy that were central to past successes—for example, in civil and women's rights. "In the 21st century, the march isn't the vehicle," as a recent blog entry put it in the *Stanford Social Innovation Review*. "Social entrepreneurs are basically revolutionaries but are too practical to be placard-carrying types," says Pamela Hartigan, the director of the Skoll Centre for Social Entrepreneurship at

Oxford University.[14] It's a good job that her sisters in the struggle for the vote didn't heed this misleading advice. Demonstrations frighten business and governments more than they admit, and those who participate are often changed in ways that stay with them throughout their lives.

Control, Speed, and Scale

To many philanthrocapitalists, I'll venture, the world is a giant machine in which levers can be pulled to achieve the desired result, not an organic entity that is constantly evolving—unpredictable and uncontrollable, where there are few right answers and past success is rarely a reliable guide to action in the future. And I think that underpins their fascination with predetermined metrics and objectives. Perhaps that's why the "Sage of Omaha," Warren Buffett, once told an interviewer to "beware of geeks bearing formulas."

At first I was mystified by the philanthrocapitalists' obsession with control and micromanagement, packaging everything into neat and tidy boxes that can be assigned a name and number so that we can save the world for $1.23 per head, not $1.31. This seems so backward in a world that prides itself on innovation. But having delved a little more deeply, I think it is perfectly understandable, because in business, losing control over all the details is seen as a path to waste, inefficiency, and failure. Tight discipline must be exerted down the chain of supply to control for quality and price. There's nothing wrong with that, unless you also apply the same thinking in the world of collective action, democratic negotiation, and empowerment.

In business, the pressure to scale up production quickly is natural, even imperative, because that is how unit costs decline and profit margins grow; but in civil society, things have to move at the pace required by social transformation, which is generally slow because it is so complex and conflicted. Having inherited their wealth or made it very quickly, the philanthro-capitalists are not in the mood to wait around for their results. In business, scaling up tends to be direct, through more consumers and larger markets; in civil society, scale tends to come through indirect strategies that change policies, regulations, values, and institutions—for example, the rules within which individual producers operate in order to generate a bigger, systemic impact. Business wants smooth distribution, quick payment, and high volumes in order to maximize returns; civil society might focus on small numbers of people and their concerns, which are rarely if ever smooth.

Citizens' groups get results by giving things away, diffusing ideas and values through networks and movements, and cooperating with many best providers. By contrast, the logic of the market is to hold things back in order to gain a competitive advantage, and results are focused on each firm. Citizens' groups may get smaller or larger, or even disappear, without this being seen as failure. And social transformation requires humility, patience, and the determination to hang in there for the very long term—a mirror image of the impatience and short-term thinking that drive most markets and entrepreneurs. Finally, business systems for monitoring and measurement are too bureaucratic and time-consuming for most nonprofits, amassing unnecessary quantities of information that are never used and tying up staff resources. If, as the rhetoric suggests, the philanthrocapitalists want nonprofits to be self-reliant, to stand on their own two feet, and to "help people help themselves," then they can't simultaneously shower nonprofit organizations with predetermined outcomes and indicators that tie them into knots.

Business Metrics and Democratic Accountability

As we all get into bed together through blurring, blending, hybrids, and public-private partnerships, what happens to accountability and to the role of citizens' groups in promoting checks and balances? Who wants a system with no separation of powers, especially given the unequal power and resources of civil society and business? Privatizing the resolution of social problems takes decision making out of the public domain and potentially takes considerations of the public interest off the table with it. As a *New York Times* editorial put it, "Public spending is allocated democratically among competing demands, whereas rich benefactors can spend on anything they want, and they tend to spend on projects close to their hearts."[15] Some philanthrocapitalists are beginning to respond to this challenge by becoming more transparent and soliciting feedback from their grantees. The Gates Foundation, for example, has asked for feedback from children and teachers in schools that receive funding through its Youth Truth program, but listening to your beneficiaries is a pretty anodyne version of the *democratic* accountability structures that mark out the strongest citizens' groups, such as Make the Road New York, whose work was highlighted in chapter 1. It is a membership group whose staff members are held accountable to low-income and immigrant constituencies; and that builds the strength and relevance of the organization, and boosts its social and political impact. Not all civil society groups have members, elections, and the like, but even those that don't have them need to be in constant touch with the people whom they serve.

Business metrics and measures of success privilege size, growth, and market share, as opposed to the quality of interactions between people in civil society and the capacities and

institutions they help to create. These are measures of linear
change—getting more results within the systems that exist—not
measures of transformation. When investors evaluate a business, they ultimately need to answer only one question: How
much money will it make? The equivalent for civil society is
the social impact that organizations might achieve, alone and
together, but that is much more difficult to evaluate, especially at the deeper levels of social change. As Jim Collins of *Good
to Great* fame puts it, money is an input to citizens' groups, not
a "measure of greatness." And although work is being done to
quantify the "social rate of return" from investments in citizen
action, this is extremely difficult to do (perhaps impossible in
any rigorous way), leaving philanthrocapitalists to rely on mea-
suring the *economic* benefits that derive from projects that create
employment, housing, and the like. "The reason the nonprofit sector exists at all is because it can fund and invest in social
issues that the for-profit market can't touch because they can't
be measured," says Paul Shoemaker, director of Social Venture
Partners International in Seattle. "The nonprofit market is not
designed to be 'efficient' that way. Yet we're applying the same
efficiency metrics to both sectors."

In civil society, processes, values, capacities, relationships,
and the depth of engagement with other institutions may be
more important as measures of impact than tangible outputs
or the direct products of each organization; and impact relies
on forces—such as government action—that are usually out of
their control. Yet how does one measure these things and the
independence, capacity, and connectedness of communities that
are their ultimate objectives? There are no standard metrics for
caring, solidarity, compassion, tolerance, and mutual support.
For many activists and volunteers, participation *is* the objective, not some predetermined indicator of success—their goal

is their *role* as citizens active in their communities, whatever the problems they have to confront. And even if you could find measures for things like empowerment, it wouldn't mean that one organization should necessarily be supported over others, because two nonprofits working in the same community could be active with different people, in different settings, and with different methodologies and styles. Civil society benefits from having lots of groups doing similar things in loose association with one another. That's why its ecosystems are so important.

In other words, civil society and the market are different, and citizens' groups that dilute their identity will lose their most precious asset—public trust and credibility. Opinion polls on both sides of the Atlantic show that members of the public rank authenticity higher than professionalism in the qualities they want to see. Most people *want* nonprofits to preserve their distinct identity and value the differences that separate them from business.[16] Otherwise, what's the point of having a civil society at all?

Meeting Grounds and Markets

Philanthrocapitalists claim that *social capital markets*, as they call them, will separate effective and ineffective organizations by forcing nonprofits to compete with each other for resources, allocated by investors according to common metrics of efficiency and impact. Believers in this school of thought therefore emphasize the collection of data and its storage on the World Wide Web, so that those who want to give to charity have more information to guide their decisions—from sites like Guide-Star International,[17] for example, and New Philanthropy Capital (NPC) in London.[18] There is nothing inherently wrong in this—in fact, these Web sites can be very useful to those who don't know the field. The problems come when standardized metrics are used to evaluate and rank different organizations, which may then push resources to some at the expense of others. Neither GuideStar nor NPC is doing this, but others are getting pretty close.

Pulse, for example, was developed by the Acumen Fund, a venture philanthropy group, with help from Google. It provides a common framework that allows users to "manage financial and non-financial metrics through a user-configurable, open source XBRL-enabled toolset," which should come in handy the next time the Ladies Auxiliary asks you to donate to its latest pancake breakfast. These metrics are supposed to cover "social and environmental impact." Yet, apart from a mention of board diversity and a few other indicators of which parts of the population benefit along the way, there is nothing social about them at all—just a long list of quantitative indicators that describe such things as the numbers of people served, the demographics of the population, and the amount of money spent. Empowerment, participation, values, capacities, relationships, community cohesion, and everything else that is genuinely social is nowhere to be seen.[19]

Or take GiveWell, launched by Holden Karnofsky and Elie Hassenfeld, both twenty-six years young. They left their jobs at a hedge fund to launch a new ratings agency in New York that "studies non-profits in particular fields and ranks them on their effectiveness," defined as "the most lives saved for the least money," an assessment that has defeated the best social scientists for at least a hundred years. Unfortunately, the capitalist part of their philanthrocapitalist imagination proved a bit too strong. Both were caught *astroturfing*—promoting GiveWell by using fake online identities and the e-mail addresses of other people in order to drum up business for their organization.[20]

But social capital markets give rise to much more serious problems for civil society than this.

First, there are no reliable measures of the true social return on investment, only estimates of the financial value of those aspects of social change that can be quantified, which are relatively few. That's because social impact is complicated, unpredictable, and long term, so it can't be captured in a number.

Second, even if one could agree on reliable social impact metrics, how would one apply them across so many different issues and interpretations? Who is to say that saving the rainforest deserves more investment than ending gun crime or racism? Should we direct more money to apples instead of pears because some of us prefer their taste?

Third, what is counted as a cost may actually be a benefit—such as the time invested in messy and democratic decision-making processes and negotiation. Remember the Stanford study that showed that the most successful citizens' groups were the "purest, most radical, and most disorganized"? What seems effective now may prove costly in the future, and what seems costly now may yield long-term results if nonprofits stick with it over time.

Fourth, rankings imply attribution, which is impossible in the world of social change because results are never driven by one project or organization acting on its own, so who exactly is being rewarded, and is that even fair?

Fifth, differences in standard metrics may not reflect meaningful variations in performance. Two nonprofits, each working on community development, could show hugely different costs and other indicators for serving the same number of people, because one works with groups that are more difficult to engage, but it would be impossible to know that in advance.

The overall result might be to reward nonprofits for

superficial results and penalize those whose work is most important to long-term social change, especially those who do not
speak the language of venture philanthropy or who cannot meet
their demands for standard data. Is that the best way to channel
more resources to social transformation?

Blending and Blurring—Can These Differences Be Bridged?

These are deep-rooted differences, but are they unbridgeable,
frozen forever in some mutually antagonistic embrace? Philanthrocapitalism answers this question with a loud and emphatic
no; social enterprise, venture philanthropy, and corporate social
responsibility have staked their future on the claim that different values and philosophies can be brought together to mutual
advantage, but are they correct?

Let's start by acknowledging that all organizations produce
different kinds of value in varying proportions—financial, social,
and environmental—whether they are citizens' groups or businesses. This is the foundation for Jed Emerson's Blended Value
Proposition, which has been very influential among the philanthrocapitalists. These proportions can be changed (or *blended*)
through conscious or unplanned action, but not without real
implications for those forms of value that are reduced, chal-
lenged, or contradicted in return, and that's where the proposition begins to unravel. I'm no mathematician, but I know that
I can't give more than 100 percent to anything at any point in
time, so if 60 percent is taken up with financial concerns, then
only 40 percent remains. Is 40 percent enough to achieve the
social impact that I want, or should it be 60 percent or more?
Which blends are effective in work for social transformation
and which are not—strong and weak, corporate, fair trade and

organic? Does one set of values become diluted or polluted when you mix it with the others? Is the resulting cocktail taste-less—like mixing wine and vinegar—or delicious, a margar-ita made in heaven? And are there some things—like oil and water—that do not mix at all?

As I've already pointed out, competition and coopera-tion, self-interest and sacrifice, individualism and collective action—these are not natural bedfellows who sleep comfortably together at night, and only when we are honest about this prob-lem can successful partnerships be formed. Discussions of blend-ed value seem to take place in a world free of trade-offs, costs, and contradictions, yet the experiments described in chapter 3 all revealed that mission and the market are in constant tension with each other. Although it's possible to get more social val-ue against the financial bottom line when providing goods and services, the desire to make a profit always imposes restrictions on the deeper social impact of an organization and its work. This is especially true for civil society groups that have noth-ing to sell or trade—they *are* their social value, and the conse-quences of seeing it eroded could be calamitous. One can and should debate these costs and trade-offs, decide whether they are acceptable, and manage them with more or less success, but one cannot ignore that they exist.

History shows that organizations that started with a social purpose steadily lost it as they became more embedded in the market. This was the experience of many of the cooperatives, credit unions, and mutual-aid societies that flourished in Europe in the nineteenth and twentieth centuries. They were certain-ly blending value, but over time, one type of value tended to squeeze out the others. A contemporary example would be Fred-die Mac and Fannie Mae, the U.S. mortgage providers that suffered so much in the financial crisis that they also helped to cause. Because Freddie Mac and Fannie Mae were hybrid public-private ventures with a social mission, investors assumed that the government would always make good on their debts, so both agencies borrowed money more cheaply than their competitors and used it to issue mortgages that were far too risky. What was supposed to be a positive blend turned out to have significant costs, with neither the financial discipline of markets, nor the oversight of government, nor the values of civil society to correct them or at least blow the whistle.

It's because of these problems that collaboration among separate organizations may be better than blending or competition. It preserves the difference and independence required to secure real change in markets (not just extend their social reach), and to support the transition to transformative approaches that might deliver long-lasting social impact. And it restricts business influence to the two areas where these differences can be bridged with manageable social costs. The first is delivering social and environmental services—the core of social enterprise and the prime focus for most venture philanthropy investments. This approach is sound because it supports markets to do what they are good at but with more of a social twist, and it doesn't encourage businesses to stray into territory where they have no competence or expertise. The second is strengthening the financial management of nonprofit organizations, especially those that have something to sell or trade in the market. If you do want to raise commercial revenue, you obviously need to understand how the market works and how best to engage with it. These are not skills that most nonprofits have, so one would expect that business should be able to help them, perhaps creating some spillover effects in the process that strengthen their social mission.

Apart from these two areas, there is little to support the view that philanthrocapitalism will save the world, and too many of its adherents are stuck at the low-impact end of the spectrum outlined in chapter 2, wedded to the use of market mechanisms and values where this makes little sense, and seemingly oblivious to the damage they may be doing to civil society and to the human values that animate social transformation. Approaches to resolving social and moral questions through markets and other means have traditionally been seen as different, separate, and sometimes deliberately antagonistic. There have been many hybrids, and there will be many more in the future, but they always encounter trade-offs and contradictions in their work. That's a strong argument for concluding that continued separation—though working together in complementary ways—is a better way forward than blending together elements from these very different worlds.

I think that difference is something to be celebrated and protected, not squeezed out by competition in social capital markets or imprisoned in some people's conception of how nonprofits should perform. In fact, it's the difference that *makes* the difference to social transformation—the fact that societies have counterweights to business thinking, and places where different values and motivations can survive. That is presumably why Jim Collins, in a pamphlet that seems conspicuous by its absence among the philanthrocapitalists, given his stature in the corporate world, concludes that "we must reject the idea—well-intentioned, but dead wrong—that the primary path to greatness in the social sectors is to become more like a business."[21]

CHAPTER FIVE

The Difference That Makes the Difference

 The Decline of Philanthrocapitalism and the Rise of Citizen Philanthropy

Philanthrocapitalism offers one way to increase the social impact of the modern market economy, by altering incentives and giving more back through foundations and corporate social responsibility, but there are other approaches to changing the ways that wealth is produced and distributed which might achieve even better results. Traditionally, societies have used corporate taxation, government regulation, and civil society pressure to force business to reform. Recently, advocates of new business models, community-based economics, and other radical innovations have pressed for more fundamental changes in ownership and governance that would alter the whole basis on which markets currently work. In both of these cases, real transformation occurs when business behaves more like civil society, not the other way around. I suspect that civil society will be able to push business further in this direction from a position of diversity and strength. It's the difference that *makes* the difference to society, let's remember, so working together but independently may be a better way forward than dissolving our differences in some soggy middle ground. In the real world, there is no seamless weaving of competition and cooperation, doing good and doing well, sacrifice and self-interested behavior. If something seems too good to be true—like securing social justice by becoming a billionaire—then it almost certainly is. Philanthrocapitalism is an interesting idea, but there's no evidence to support the wilder claims that are made for its influence and impact, and little logic that demonstrates why business thinking should be more effective than other approaches to fostering social change.

The leaders of this movement want civil society to become more like a business, but I think it is just as likely that philanthrocapitalist experiments will end up as a subset of the market, doing work that is useful but limited, and leaving citizens' groups to build on the distinctive strengths and values of voluntary citizen action. And that really is OK. In fact, less of a focus on saving the world and more of a commitment to being useful where that makes sense would be a cause for quiet celebration. Using the market to increase access to useful goods and services, fostering healthy and sustainable economic solutions, and adopting the kind of total corporate social responsibility described in chapter 2 would all help to lay the groundwork for social transformation, and make it much easier for government and civil society to complete the job. After all, the theory of *comparative advantage* is a core part of any business textbook: focus on what you do best and leave the rest to others. If this theory works for markets and for trade, why doesn't business respect the appropriate division of labor when it comes to social change? And if business doesn't focus on its areas of real expertise, it will inevitably be ineffective, waste resources, and see its image tarnished somewhere along the way.

So what's the bottom line? Mike Lee puts it this way in his blog on Social Edge: "Business is a tool for change, not a comprehensive way of looking at the world or treating other human beings."[1] The hyperagency of the philanthrocapitalists has to be balanced by ordinary people's agency, expressed through civil society and through their elected representatives in government, lest everything be privatized and taken over by the ideas and priorities of the few. If philanthrocapitalism is firmly but respectfully put in its place, more oxygen will be available to breathe new life into older institutions, so that government, business, and civil society can play on a level field and not one dominated by market forces. *Citizen philanthropy*—broad based, deep rooted, bottom up, passionate, and uncontrolled—would provide a much stronger foundation for social transformation than reliance on business and the market. It might even allow us to return to philanthropy's original meaning as "love of humankind."

If I were ever invited to address the philanthrocapitalists, what would I say? "First, a big vote of thanks for taking up the challenge of entrepreneurship for the public good. Without your efforts, we wouldn't be having this debate, and the world would be further from the commercial and technological advances required to cure malaria and get microcredit to everyone who needs it. But don't stop there. Please use your wealth and influence to bring about deeper transformations in systems and in structures, be open to learning from civil society and not just teaching it the virtues of business thinking, measure the costs as well as the benefits of your investments and interventions, learn more rigorously from history, and redirect your resources to groups and innovations that will change society forever, including the economic system that has made you rich. That's not too much to ask for, is it?" Well, perhaps it is. None of these things are high on the philanthrocapitalist agenda, because they would transform the economic system completely and lead to a radically different distribution of its benefits and costs. Nevertheless, if the rich genuinely want to save the world, then an honest consideration of these challenges is the best place to start.

Billionaires are pragmatic people, with little appetite, I'll wager, for abstract arguments about long-term transformation when there are so many immediate problems to be solved. That's fair enough, I think. Pragmatism is a feature of civil society too, and neither wants to make the best the enemy of the good. Small victories are still victories, and a vaccine against HIV/AIDS would be a very big victory indeed. Yet compared with the size and complexity of the problems facing the world, the contributions of civil society and government, and the impact that business could make if it fixed itself instead of focusing on fixing others, philanthrocapitalism is small change.

I'm quite sure that most philanthrocapitalists want to make a bigger difference and learn how that might happen. After all, they are successful and energetic people, and no one is forcing Gates, Skoll, and the rest to give billions of dollars away (they could have kept it for themselves), so there is plenty of room for improvement through dialogue and learning. "I don't believe there is a for-profit answer to everything," says Pierre Omidyar, "but if for-profit capital can do more good than it does today, foundations can concentrate their resources where they are most needed," a welcome dose of common sense in a conversation dominated by hype.[2] "What I long to do," says Bill Clinton, "is to see this [approach] integrated into every philanthropic activity *where it is appropriate*[my italics]," and "where it is appropriate" may be a small but not unimportant part of the picture as a whole.[3] "Are we creating world peace or fundamentally changing the world?" asks Mark Shuttleworth, the South African billionaire backer of open source software such as Ubuntu. "No, but we could shift . . . the amount of innovation per dollar they expect."[4] So how can we cooperate in moving forward together, and what can ordinary people do to help?

Organizing an Honest and Open Conversation

The first priority is to pause, take a very deep breath, and create space for a different kind of conversation. Philanthrocapitalism is seductive for many different reasons—the allure of a new magic bullet, set against the reality of plodding along, step by step, in the swamps of social change; the glitz and glamour of gaining entry to a new global elite; and the promise of maintaining a system that made you rich and powerful while you simultaneously pursue the public good. We all want our place in history as the ones who saved the world, but this is surely immature. Will "social enterprise end up intoxicated by virtue, breathing its own exhaust," as a report from SustainAbility in London concluded?[5] There is always a danger of too much self-reinforcement when new ideas make big claims, and challenges are sometimes met with a prickly or hostile response, especially when the claimants are used to being lionized for their achievements. "Everything short of a *fatwa*" was the response of a leader from European venture philanthropy when I asked him how his colleagues had reacted to an earlier version of this book. And NCRP (the National Committee for Responsive Philanthropy), in Washington, D.C., was showered with vitriolic criticism when it dared to enter the fray in 2009. Paul Brest, the president of the William and Flora Hewlett Foundation in California, spends much of his time advising others on how to make their giving more effective by using logic models, social capital markets, and other ideas inspired by business thinking; yet when NCRP issued its own criteria for "Philanthropy at Its Best," it was labeled "presumptuous," "Orwellian," and "breathtakingly arrogant" on his blog.[6]

What crime did NCRP commit to warrant this reaction? It recommended that foundations "contribute more resources to a strong, participatory democracy that engages all communities, by providing at least half their grant-making dollars to benefit lower-income communities and other marginalized groups." It suggested that foundations "invest in the health of nonprofit partners by providing at least fifty percent of those dollars for general operating support." And it asked that foundations "demonstrate more transparency and accountability to the public, partly by increasing the diversity of their boards."[7] This hardly seems like heresy, and the percentages are fairly arbitrary, for sure, but the thinking that underlies them is important, even if it deviates from the orthodoxy of business-is-always-best. Perhaps it's time to launch a slow food movement for the philanthrocapitalists in order to help them savor the complexities of what's involved and the subtle flavors that others bring to the table. It's not that our old ideas about social transformation were perfect; it's that our new ideas are imperfect, too, and almost certainly won't turn out as planned. There is no place for triumphalism in this conversation. Instead, let's have a full-throated public debate to sort out the claims of both philanthrocapitalists and their critics, and to inform the huge expansion of philanthropy that is projected over the next forty years.

Some people think this is unnecessarily divisive. Let's move beyond sterile debates about for-profit *or* not-for-profit activity, and just accept that we all agree on meeting in the middle. Except that we don't all agree, and in fact I start from the opposite assumption: Philanthrocapitalism is a controversial movement that ought to be interrogated, since only then can one identify where business and the market can be helpful to social change and when they can't. So here's the $55 trillion question, the amount of money that is expected to be passed between generations in the United States alone over the next forty years: Will these vast resources be used to pursue social transformation, or will they be frittered away in spending on the symptoms, or could they actually make things worse?[8] The stakes are very high, so why not organize a series of dialogues between philanthrocapitalists and their critics, on condition that they shed the mock civility that turns honest conversation into Jell-O? There isn't much point in staying in the comfort zone, forever apart in different camps, like the World Economic Forum and the World Social Forum, which take place in splendid isolation every year. Deep-rooted differences about capitalism and social change are unlikely to go away, so let's have more honesty and dissent before consensus, so that it might actually be meaningful when it arrives.

Effective philanthropists do learn from their experience and the conversations they have with others. Melinda Gates, for example, describes this process well: "Why do something about vaccines but nothing about clean water? Why work on tuberculosis but not on agricultural productivity? Why deliver mosquito nets but not financial services?"[9] Of course, there is another set of questions waiting to be answered at an even deeper level: Why work on agricultural productivity but not on rights to land? Why work on financial services but not on changing the economic system in which they sit? But these are challenges that face all foundations and they are best addressed together, because all of us have much to learn from others. Rather than assuming that business provides the answers, why not put all the questions on the table and allow all sides to have their assumptions tested? Who knows—this kind of conversation might lead us far beyond the current debate to envision a more effective system for financing social change that transcends the limitations of *all* existing approaches to philanthropy.

Reforming Philanthropy for Social Transformation

If philanthrocapitalism doesn't provide the answers, how should societies finance successful social change? Perhaps the only answer that different camps agree on is "not with the system we have today," an ineffective patchwork quilt of public and private funding that is full of gaps and imperfections. If we were to rebuild this system, I'd suggest a few guiding principles. First, involve as many people as possible so that everyone can share in defining which problems get addressed, and how. This is fundamental to the workings of any just and democratic society. Second, put those at the sharp end of social problems at the center of the system rather than on the periphery, where they stand now. Those who experience poverty and dispossession should be the prime movers in identifying where additional resources can be helpful in finding and implementing solutions. Third, make the system as non-bureaucratic as possible, so that resources can be secured without nonprofits' jumping through so many hoops. Fourth, find ways of directing as many resources as possible to the most difficult and entrenched social problems, since that's where government and business usually fear to tread. And finally, strengthen transparency, accountability, and learning, so that peer and public pressure can encourage innovation without the need for too much government intervention.

This is a road map for replacing noblesse oblige with citizen-centered philanthropy, strongly linked to the revival of broad-based civil society activism as the wellspring of social transformation. The best form of philanthropy has got to be

philanthropy that addresses the conditions that make it necessary in the first place—using the wealth of the world in order
to transform it, not simply to ameliorate the symptoms of social
problems. Philanthropy as we know it now (or at least that part
of it that is institutionalized in foundations) is based on a strange
assumption: Let's develop a hugely costly and divisive system
for creating wealth, and then hope that those who benefit most
will give some back to solve problems that they have helped to
create. That's probably the least efficient way possible of tackling social problems, so why not reform the system itself so that
it can be proactive in supporting more fundamental change?

Strengthening Transparency and Accountability

"They're called the Good Club—and they want to save the
world . . . the tiny global elite of billionaire philanthropists who
recently held their first and highly secretive meeting in the heart
of New York City."[10] With secrecy like that, it's not surprising
that public opinion is suspicious of foundations, which play by
their own rules and operate largely outside the realm of accountability. As long as they maintain a governing board, obey the
law, and file some basic information with their regulators, they
can do whatever they like. In theory, that gives them the freedom to take risks and invest in unpopular causes, but in practice it can stifle openness to learning, challenge, and change,
especially when boards of directors are drawn from the same
small circles or limited to members of the founder's family and
their friends. You can even leave all your money to your dogs
and still lower the taxes on your estate, as Leona Helmsley did
when she died in 2007. The hotel queen's actions may be an
extreme example, but if philanthropy is private funding in the
public interest, it doesn't seem unreasonable to insist that the

public has some say in defining how its interests are identified and addressed. Currently there is no way to do this. Philanthropy reduces the tax bill of anyone who makes a donation, but it also reduces the resources that governments have to pursue the public good (to the tune of $40 billion in the United States in 2006 alone). Only 11 percent of the money that Americans give to charity addresses social justice, so this is far from an academic issue.[11] The question is more pressing for living donors who have tied their business interests to their philanthropy in ways that might benefit themselves—by reducing their own tax liabilities, for example, boosting the revenue of their companies, or improving their image among consumers.

If my government doesn't do what it is supposed to do, then I can hold it accountable by voting in a new one. If Bill Gates does something I don't like, there's nothing I can do because he's a private citizen in charge of his own foundation. However, Gates is as big an influence on global health and education policy as any government, and the decisions he makes will affect the lives of millions. It's great that he and other philanthrocapitalists want to improve public schools in America, but why should his ideas about how to accomplish that task win out over others just because he's rich? Is it desirable that a foundation governed by a board of three family members is able to play such an influential role, or to decide that health outranks global warming as the number one priority? That was the question raised in 2008 by a World Health Organization official, who complained that it was no longer possible to find independent reviewers for research proposals because they were all on the payroll of the Gates Foundation.[12] Sour grapes, perhaps, but he has a point. Philanthropy has always been an expression of individual desires, and it is assumed that those desires are supportive of more broadly shared visions of social change. If they are not, societies may be in trouble as philanthropy continues to expand.

How might these accountability problems be addressed? Some obvious measures could be taken without reducing the freedom of philanthropists to support work as they wish—for example, passing legislation to protect the public interest in schemes for embedded giving like Project Red, in which a proportion of the price of goods and services is donated to social causes; in for-profit fund-raising, where the fund-raisers often take the lion's share of the resources; in the use of charitable trusts so that they genuinely benefit the public and are not simply a way of avoiding paying taxes; and in other forms of business involvement in philanthropy. There is also no reason why foundations should not be obliged to release more information to the public on what they are doing and why, beyond the limited financial and salary data that are currently published in reports to government regulators. Why not require all foundations to compile a publicly available summary of their program evaluations every five years, and to solicit feedback from grantees and from independent experts in the field? How about town-hall meetings in communities where foundations are particularly active? Why not commission independent impact studies for any tax-exempt activity above a certain size, and publish the results?

More controversially, I'd suggest a new legal requirement for the nation's largest foundations to report on the results of their work to Congress or Parliament every five years as part of a nationwide foundation summit, open to public and media participation. Such a move would be vigorously rejected by many foundation leaders who are fearful of government regulation, and that's perfectly understandable. But if other institutions in society must explain themselves to our elected representatives, it is difficult to see why foundations should be excluded. No doubt these objections will continue, but foundations cannot seriously object to more investment in research and evaluation that measures progress on the important questions. Do philanthropy, social enterprise, and corporate social responsibility reduce or reinforce inequalities of wealth and power? And when the hype and self-promotion are peeled back, what of substance remains? Answering those questions requires more social science and less of an obsession with financial metrics. That is accountancy, not accountability, and it does little to measure long-term social change. Why not dedicate 10 percent of annual foundation payout to increasing the resources and capacities devoted to learning in philanthropy, and protect half of that amount for joint learning with those actually doing social change work on the ground?

Long-term action learning is particularly important for shedding more light on civil society's changing shape, for testing whether the ecosystem effects I mentioned in chapter 3 are as damaging as I've claimed, and for evaluating the social impact of philanthrocapitalism in all its different guises. What we have right now are anecdotes, self-serving studies, and a few rigorous accounts of what is happening on the ground. The "Inquiry into the Future of Civil Society in the UK and Ireland" (sponsored by the Carnegie UK Trust) is a good example of the kind of work that is required, involving large numbers of people *in* civil society in reflecting critically on their work and how it is being affected by current trends in politics, the economy, and the environment; supporting exercises in "future visioning" so that new alliances and coalitions can be born; and commissioning independent research on how civil society groups can make more of a difference to the big issues of the future, such as climate change and the shape of the emerging social economy.[13]

All this rests on finding better metrics to inform decision making that measure progress toward short- and long-term social change *together*, like those used by SCOPE, SPARC, and Make the Road New York that were cited in chapter 1. This is likely to be more fruitful than the endless refinement of *financial* measures of social value. Social capital markets might work for "social businesses," as Muhammad Yunus calls them—groups that compete to deliver the same goods and services in well-defined sectors of the market. But elsewhere in civil society, we need more meeting grounds than markets—places, both real and virtual, where nonprofits and their supporters can forge long-term relationships with each other, experiment with different ideas about impact measurement and performance, and generate diverse revenue streams without incurring the costs of over-competition or being shoehorned into a narrow definition of success. Why not sponsor immersion trips so that funders can learn about the realities of power and the politics of social transformation from those at the sharp end of this process (and not from the ghastly stage-managed versions beloved of foundations and their trustees)? These trips should also include the new breed of donor-advisers, such as Fidelity and McKinsey and Company, as they are playing an increasingly important role in directing philanthropy in one way or another. Yet with some notable exceptions, they all come from a business or investment background and have little experience in the world of social change. Think how much more could be achieved with an education of this kind, given that many philanthrocapitalists are in their thirties and forties and will enjoy even greater access to resources as they grow older.

Citizen Philanthropy

Reforms in transparency and accountability will only go so far in inducing and incentivizing the changes that philanthropy requires. Can philanthropy be transformed "from a top-down process into an invitation for the grassroots to speak up and make something happen"? Yes, through citizen philanthropy, says Peter Deitz, the founder of Social Actions. "The new philanthropy doesn't require millionaires, corporate social responsibility programs, or large endowments to run. Instead, it runs on the resources and passions of real people. No one owns it but everyone can participate."[14] That's an attractive proposition, reflecting a wider change in the economy to democratize how goods and services are produced (for example, open source software), and potentially underwriting a rebirth of broad-based civil society activism by diffusing power and responsibility away from a few giant foundations. Philanthropy should be a support system, not a control system, for broad-based social change.

That objective could be fostered by encouraging all foundations to spend more of their resources on increasing the power and voice of those left outside the mainstream; strengthening community organizing and broad-based social movements; and investing in poor people's capacity to change the systems and structures that keep them in their place. A meager 8 percent of philanthropic resources in the United States is currently spent on programs defined as for "public and societal benefit," as opposed to religion, opera, and the like, a figure that falls to 7 percent for money that is channeled to "communities of color" and rises to 11 percent for "social justice grant making."[15] As far as I can tell, philanthrocapitalism is doing little to change these appalling statistics, so here's a radical idea: Why not reorganize philanthropy around the one thing that civil society needs—as much money as possible with the fewest strings attached, so that the nonprofits that want it can get on with doing what they do best? That means promoting the long-term financial independence of civil society organizations through long-term unrestricted or core support; nonprofit reserve funds; and endowments and foundations controlled by disadvantaged groups themselves, such as the Dalit Foundation for so-called untouchables in India, or the First Nations Fund for Native Americans in the United States, or the growing network of women's funds that is spreading across the world. Thus far, philanthrocapitalists have made few investments in foundations like these, but they represent tremendous value for money because they pull in more resources and place those resources under direct community control.

In addition, why not expand community foundations or set up five hundred local social investment funds across the United States with $100 million each, with private contributions matched dollar for dollar by the U.S. government, or financed through civil society investment bonds or other public offerings? They could be governed by a cross-section of representatives from civil society, government, and business who were elected or selected from their constituencies, a model that has already been successfully tried out in the world of foreign aid. This would get resources much closer to where they are most needed and build local accountability for results. Economic security for those doing the hardest work on the front lines of social change could be fostered by dramatically expanding health care and pensions for community organizers and other civil society activists, which foundations could fund by pooling their resources under one or more of the programs that already operate among nonprofits but on much too small a scale. And how about scaling up support for free communications and the infrastructure of the public sphere—the community radio stations, newspapers, investigative journalists, electronic media, and face-to-face debates that are essential to stir up the world of philanthropy and get more people involved?

Additional tax breaks for small contributions, and for nonprofits that raise money from their members and from broad swaths of the population (not just from foundations, large donors, and fee-for-service payments), might encourage civil society groups to return to their roots and strengthen their democratic effects, in the same way that President Obama's election campaign drew strength from large numbers of small donations, 90 percent of which were for $100 or less—but obviously directed at nonpartisan organizations and causes. Evidence suggests that this is also an effective way of linking philanthropy to civic and political activism (including higher rates of voting), rather than just writing checks and clicking on a Web site. Foundations could also reduce the transaction costs of getting support, especially for groups that are less well-resourced, by redesigning application procedures, increasing the length of grants, and finding better ways to distribute funds through multi-funder initiatives.

The absence of grass-roots voices, community organizers, and labor representatives on the boards of major foundations is quite striking, populated as they are by business leaders, CEOs of large nonprofits, and the occasional academic or other public figure. This deprives philanthropy of vital knowledge and perspectives from those at the sharp end of social change, and narrows the range of views around the table. Perhaps it is time to mandate a new legal requirement that no foundation can receive tax exemption unless its board contains some representation from the communities it claims to serve. After all, they are the subjects, not the objects, of social transformation. Those closest to the action have ideas and experiences that can shed light on problems and solutions, and they have networks and associations through which they can pull in good ideas and provide feedback to the funders. Foundation leaders will resist and complain about any requirement like this, as they did when the Greenlining Institute in Oakland suggested more diversity on boards in a report that whipped up a storm of opposition in 2008, but public and political pressure will eventually force change through.

Finally, can philanthropy be more fun? If it can't, then most people probably won't join in. Can it give as much credence to empathy and intuition, community and joy, and wild and wacky ideas as it does to the dull utility of the calculator and the spreadsheet? Can it value experience in social movements and other forms of civil society activism as much as it values management consultants and MBAs? Can it open itself up to the deep lessons of social science and history as well as to the mildly critical reports that are regularly commissioned from intermediaries at great cost and to minimal effect? Can it give support to meeting grounds where people can talk as equals, not just social capital markets that divide givers and receivers and pit one charity against another? And shouldn't we celebrate foundations that have the courage, creativity, and sticking power *not* to swallow the latest philanthropic fashion that trots down the runway, but to interrogate it ethically and empirically, and to stand their ground?

The best answer to all these questions is for you and me to get involved in a broad-based movement in support of citizen philanthropy, and to become philanthropists ourselves but do so in a way that does not reinforce or replicate the unhealthy patterns of the past; to ask the difficult questions about philanthropy and social change, and not to be brushed aside when we are told that we have no right to question foundations that belong to others; to accept the obligation to hold ourselves accountable to more than a board of close friends and acquaintances; and to see ourselves as partners in a common project of social transformation that places disadvantaged people at the center of their own story.

Philanthrocapitalism is the product of a particular era of industrial change that has brought about temporary monopolies in the systems required to operate the knowledge economy, often controlled by individuals who are able to accumulate spectacular amounts of wealth. That same era has produced great inequalities and social dislocations, and experience suggests that such wealth will be politically unsustainable unless much of it is given away, just as in earlier decades when Ford, Rockefeller, and Carnegie found themselves in much the same position. In that sense, philanthrocapitalism is a predictable outcome of today, but I doubt whether this movement and its ideology is a good guide to tomorrow and the future. I think it is much more likely that citizen philanthropy will emerge over a long period of time to dominate a landscape that is characterized by more democracy in politics and economics, and in which human values and the values of the market are held in a better and more equal balance. There are already signs that this is happening as a result of public reactions to the financial crisis that engulfed the world in 2008, in the push for new forms of economics and new business models cited in chapter 2, and in continuing attempts to deepen and reinvigorate democratic practices in societies from China to the United States.

Conclusion

No one wants to leave a legacy of small change, so even if the philanthrocapitalists are hesitant about these suggestions and the critique that lies behind them, I think that many will be prepared to join the conversation that is required to transform how social change is funded in the future. And if they are not, some unpleasant surprises may be waiting in the wings in the form of more public challenge and greater government regulation. Rising inequality and concentrated influence are politically unsustainable, as a previous generation of business leaders found to their cost in America's Gilded Age. These trends always stimulate a counter-reaction, rooted in civil society and government, to protect democracy and the deeper values that animate the popular imagination. Will the same be said of the rise and fall of the philanthrocapitalists?

Deep down, perhaps the leaders of this movement know that this is true. "Reducing inequity is the highest human achievement," said Bill Gates Jr., when he spoke at Harvard University's graduation ceremony in June 2007.[16] "The question of how to assure that American capitalism creates a decent society is one that will engage all of us in the years ahead," concludes H. Lee Scott, the CEO of Walmart.[17] So let's hold these leaders to their commitments and ensure that they deliver on their promises. Some wealthy individuals are already heading in this direction. For example, the Arcus Foundation in the United States (founded by the medical equipment entrepreneur Jon Stryker) invests in efforts to promote and protect gay and lesbian rights and other areas of social and racial justice; and the Resource Generation network works with young high-net-worth individuals to "support and challenge each other" to use their wealth to contribute to "social, racial and economic justice."[18] The Omidyar Network recently gave $2.1 million to Harvard University to "identify and adapt military tools and approaches that aim to prevent genocide." Corporate Voices for Working Families links over fifty companies that have developed family-support policies for their own workforces and that advocate together for government policies that do the same; and the Hewlett Foundation's recent gift of $113 million to create one hundred endowed chairs at the University of California, Berkeley is a great demonstration of support for *public* goods.

No *one* will "save the world," as there is no single approach or set of ideas or actors that has a monopoly on wisdom, authority, or power. Only principled collective action, openness to learning and accountability, and a willingness to change ourselves where it matters most can position societies to address their social problems. The philanthrocapitalists are not superheroes, just successful individuals who have benefited from a period of rapid economic change, often more by luck than by judgment, trying to be useful and making errors and mistakes along the way, in a world of limited knowledge and constant cultural and political flux. The only difference is that they have billions of dollars to spend and the rest of us do not. Recognizing this fact, and increasing our willingness to undertake the journey together, is the first step in recapturing philanthropy from capitalism and using it to transform the economy and revitalize civil society. Instead of fixing others, business should fix itself; and in doing so, it will increase its contribution to society enormously. That doesn't mean that business and the market are irrelevant to social change, but as with any institutions, their contributions are best directed at a subset of issues and activities that provide a partial answer to social problems.

Could it be that civil society can achieve more of an impact on capitalism by strengthening its distinctive roles and values than by blending them with business? Are civil society and business just different ways of answering similar questions about production and delivery, or are they asking different questions about society altogether? At all costs, we must avoid creating a cocktail in which civil society's influence is significantly diminished. Citizens' groups have nothing to be ashamed of in not being businesses, and everything to gain by reasserting their difference and their independence. At its best, voluntary action releases incalculable social energy—the sheer joy of collective action for the public good that is free, as far as is humanly possible, of commercial considerations and self-interest. This is surely something to preserve, build on, and extend as we edge closer to a world that can be thoroughly and comprehensively transformed.

Acknowledgments

Parts of this book were first released in a pamphlet called *Just Another Emperor? The Myths and Realities of Philanthrocapitalism*, which was published in 2008 by Demos in New York and the Young Foundation in London. I owe a special debt of thanks to Miles Rapoport at Demos and to Geoff Mulgan at the Young Foundation for their initial support, and to Tim Rusch at Demos for his subsequent help and guidance throughout the process. Thanks also to Stephen Snyder at Demos for his fact-checking skills.

Johanna Vondeling at Berrett-Koehler then suggested revising and expanding the pamphlet into a book, and she has steered the process expertly from start to finish in record time, along with her many colleagues in San Francisco. I am also grateful to the *Nonprofit Quarterly* for granting permission to use an extract from their magazine in chapter 3.

Numerous people have offered feedback on various drafts of both the pamphlet and the book, including four reviewers for Berrett-Koehler, who all offered useful and constructive suggestions, whether or not they agreed with my conclusions. I also benefited from a Simon Industrial Fellowship at the Brooks World Poverty Institute at Manchester University, which allowed me to undertake further research during the process of revision and rewriting. I would like to thank the Institute's director, Professor David Hulme, for this invaluable opportunity.

Naturally, all responsibility for the content of this book remains with me.

Finally my wife, Cora, deserves my love and gratitude for having shouldered the burden of selling our old home, renovating our new home, and moving all our possessions from one to the other while I worked to complete this book.

Michael Edwards
Swan Hill, New York
July 2009

Notes

PREFACE

1. M. Taibbi, "The Great American Bubble Machine," *Rolling Stone*, http://www.rollingstone.com/politics/story/28816321, 2008.

2. R. Reich, "A Few Hundred Supernovas," *American Prospect Online*, October 2, 2006.

CHAPTER ONE

1. M. Bishop and M. Green, *Philanthrocapitalism: How the Rich Can Save the World* (New York: Bloomsbury, 2008).

2. Cited in "The New Wave of American Philanthropy," *NonProfit Times* e-newsletter, January 7, 2007. To be fair to Bono and Bobby Shriver, Product Red is one of the better *embedded giving* schemes on the market; the term describes activities in which some of the price that consumers pay for goods and services goes to a charity or other social cause. Project Red insists on detailed contracts with companies that participate so that buyers can see how much of the price they pay will find its way to the Global Fund to Fight AIDS, Tuberculosis, and Malaria. See also S. Strom, "Charity's Share from Shopping Raises Concern," *The New York Times*, December 13, 2007.

3. Cited in W. K. Kellogg Foundation, *Blurred Boundaries and Muddled Motives: A World of Shifting Social Responsibilities* (2003), 12.

4. C. Piller, "Buffet Rebuffs Efforts to Rate Corporate Conduct," *Los Angeles Times*, May 7, 2007.

5. "Richard C. Morais on Philanthropy," Forbes.com, December 23, 2007.

6. A. Clark, "Slumping Billionaires," *Guardian*, March 12, 2009.

7. M. Bishop, "The Business of Giving," *Economist*, February 19, 2006.

8. K. Hoffman, letter to the *Guardian*, April 18, 2008.

9. S. Strom, "Wall Street Fraud Leaves Charities Reeling," *New York Times*, December 16, 2008.

10. R. Shiller, *Irrational Exuberance*, 2nd ed. (New York: Broadway Business, 2006).

11. Cited in "The Business of Giving," *Economist*, February 19, 2006.

12. Clinton Global Initiative, press release, December 3, 2008, http://www .clintonglobalinitiative.org/Page.aspx?pid=3073.

13. K. Boudreaux and T. Cowen, "The Micro-Magic of Microcredit," *Wilson Quarterly*, July 14, 2008.

14. K. Heim, "Making a Profit While Helping the Poor," *Seattle Times*, May 2, 2007.

15. M. Bishop, "What Is Philanthrocapitalism?" *Alliance*, March 2007.

16. J. Novogratz, "Meeting Urgent Needs with Patient Capital," *Innovations*, vol. 2, issue 1/2 (2007): 19–30.

17. For a good account of this approach, see S. Paperin, "Philanthropy's Business Benefit," openDemocracy, April 16, 2008, http://www .opendemocracy.net.

18. P. Sellers, "Melinda Gates Goes Public," CNNMoney.com, January 7, 2008.

19. SCOPE, http://www.scopela.org.

20. Make the Road New York, http://www.maketheroadny.org.

21. SPARC, http://www.sparcindia.org.

22. Cited in an e-mail from Joel Bolnick to SDI members, January 9, 2008.

23. Movement Strategy Center, http://www.movementstrategy.org.

CHAPTER TWO

1. J. Trexler, "Social Entrepreneurship as an Algorithm: Is Social Enterprise Sustainable?" *E:CO*, vol. 10, issue 3 (2008): 65–85.

2. This was the definition used by the London-based School for Social Entrepreneurs, set up by Michael Young in the mid-1990s, http://www .sse.org.uk.

3. D. Bornstein, *How to Change the World: Social Entrepreneurs and the Power of New Ideas* (Oxford: Oxford University Press, 2004), 1.

4. J. Emerson, "The Blended Value Proposition: Integrating Social and Financial Returns," *California Management Review*, vol. 45, no. 4 (2003): 35–51; and Trexler, "Social Entrepreneurship as an Algorithm."

5. L. Foster, "A Businesslike Approach to Charity," *Financial Times*, December 10, 2007.

6. S. Strom, "Philanthropy Google's Way," *New York Times*, September 14, 2006.

7. R. John, *Venture Philanthropy: The Evolution of High-Engagement Philanthropy in Europe* (Oxford: Skoll Center for Social Entrepreneurship, 2002).

8. P. Frumkin, *Strategic Giving: The Art and Science of Philanthropy* (Chicago: Chicago University Press, 2006), 289.

9. S. Zadek, *The Civil Corporation* (London: Earthscan, 2007).

10. A term coined by Frank Dixon and his colleagues at Innovest Strategic Value Advisers.

11. B Corporation, http://www.bcorporation.net.

12. P. Barnes, *Capitalism 3.0: A Guide to Reclaiming the Commons* (San Francisco: Berrett-Koehler Publishers, 2006).

13. C. Piller, E. Sanders, and R. Dixon, "Dark Cloud over the Good Works of the Gates Foundation," *Los Angeles Times*, January 7, 2007.

14. J. Paskin, "Markets with a Social Mission," *Ode Magazine*, May 2009.

15. J. R. Bellerby, *The Contributive Society* (Oxford: Oxford Education Services, 1931).

16. *The Nonprofit Sector in Brief: Facts and Figures from the Nonprofit Almanac* (Washington, D.C.: Urban Institute, 2007).

17. National Philanthropic Trust: Philanthropy Statistics 2008, http://www.nptrust.org/philanthropy.

18. Urban Institute, 2007.

19. B. Clinton, *Giving: How Each of Us Can Change the World* (New York: Knopf, 2007), 13.

20. Sellers, "Melinda Gates Goes Public."

21. Estimates of future giving vary widely, but the latest figures give up to $21.2 trillion in "charitable bequests," $41 trillion in "accumulated assets passed to the next generation," and $55.4 trillion in "total charitable donations" in the United States between 1998 and 2055. National Philanthropic Trust, "Philanthropy Statistics," http://www.nptrust.org/philanthropy/philanthropy_stats.asp.

22. J. Emerson, "The Blended Value Map: Tracking the Intersects and Opportunities of Economic, Social and Environmental Value Creation," 2003, http://www.blendedvalue.org.

23. R. Young, "Director's Letter," *Social Enterprise Postings*, vol. 2 (Spring 2007).

24. B. Drayton, "Everyone a Changemaker: Social Entrepreneurship's Ultimate Goal," *Innovations* (Winter 2006).

25. A. Cho, "Politics, Values and Social Entrepreneurship: A Critical Appraisal," in J. Mair, ed., *Social Entrepreneurship* (Basingstoke, England: Palgrave-Macmillan, 2007).

26. J. Weisberg, "The Philanthropists' Handbook: How Billionaires Give Their Money Away," *Washington Post*, November 15, 2006.

27. *NonProfit Times* e-newsletter, January 7, 2007; remarks by Melinda French Gates, Council of Foundations, April 30, 2007.

28. J. Bendell, *Lifeworth Annual Review of Corporate Responsibility* (London: Greenleaf Publishing, 2007); J. Markoff, "Intel Quits Efforts to Get Computers to Children," *New York Times*, January 5, 2008; K. Bobo, *Wage Theft in America: Why Millions of Americans Are Not Getting Paid, and What We Can Do About It* (New York: New Press, 2008); "Mixing Politics and Wal-Mart," editorial, *New York Times*, August 16, 2008.

29. L. Wright, "Slim's Time," *New Yorker*, June 1, 2009.

30. "The Corporate Free Ride," editorial, *New York Times*, August 18, 2008; L. Browning, "Study Tallies Corporations Not Paying Income Tax," *New York Times*, August 13, 2008.

31. A. Cobham, *Tax Evasion and Tax Avoidance in Development Finance* (Oxford: Queen Elizabeth House Working Paper 129, 2006).

32. T. Macalister, "Google Is Accused of UK Tax Avoidance," *Guardian*, April 20, 2009.

33. L. Komisar, "U.S. Corporate Profits Take an Offshore Vacation," Corp-Watch, http://www.corpwatch.org/article.php?id=14392&printsafe=1 (accessed August 11, 2008).

34. G. Bedell, "The Man Giving Africa a Brighter Future," *Guardian*, February 1, 2009.

CHAPTER THREE

1. G. Gabirondo, "A New Philanthro-Capitalist Alliance in Africa?" *Pambazuka News*, April 15, 2008.

2. "Seizing the Opportunity on AIDS and Health Systems," Center for Global Development, Washington, D.C. (2008); S. Boseley, "Fighting Disease May Be Harming Global Health," *Guardian Weekly*, June 26–July 2, 2009.

3. K. Stoever, B. Karibushi, and M. Ash, "Focus on Global Health: Which Way Now?" *Alliance*, vol. 14, no. 1 (March 2009).

4. E. Flock, "How Bill Gates Blew $258 Million in India's HIV Corridor," *Business India*, June 5, 2009.

5. "Tanzania Looks beyond Free Schooling," BBC News, March 27, 2008, http://newsvote.bbc.co.uk.

6. S. Daly-Harris, cited in R. Pollin, "Micro-credit: False Hopes and Real Possibilities," *Foreign Policy in Focus*, June 21, 2007.

7. E. Malkin, "Microfinance's Success Sets Off a Debate in Mexico," *New York Times*, April 5, 2008.

8. Hudson Institute, *Index of Global Philanthropy* (Washington, D.C.: Hudson Institute, 2007).

9. C. K. Prahalad, *The Fortune at the Bottom of the Pyramid: Eradicating Poverty Through Profits* (Upper Saddle River, NJ: Wharton School Publishing, 2006).

10. A. Karnani, "Micro-finance Misses Its Mark," *Stanford Social Innovation Review* (Summer 2007): 34–40.

11. R. Tandon and J. Thekkudan, "Women's Livelihood and Global Engagement in a Globalized World" (New Delhi: PRIA and Sussex: Institute for Development Studies, 2007).

12. R. Holla and L. Menon, "Philanthrocapitalism and Corporate Social Responsibility: Do They Really Empower Civil Society?" 2008, http://www.test1.politicsofhealth.org/access/philanthro_cap.html.

13. "Response to 'The Micromagic of Microcredit,'" Woodrow Wilson International Center for Scholars, July 14, 2008, http://www.wilsoncenter.org/index.cfm?essay_id=361250&fuseaction=wq.essay.

14. *The Limits of Social Enterprise: A Field Study and Case Analysis* (New York: Seedco Policy Center, 2007).

15. C. Borzaga and J. Defourny, eds., *The Emergence of Social Enterprise* (London: Routledge, 2001); J. Mair, ed., *Social Entrepreneurship* (Basingstoke, England: Palgrave Macmillan, 2006); M. Nyssens, ed., *Social Enterprise: At the Crossroads of Market, Public Policies and Civil Society* (London: Routledge, 2006).

16. Seedco Policy Center, *The Limits of Social Enterprise*, 14–16.

17. OECD, *Reviewing OECD Experience in the Social Enterprise Sector*, report of a seminar held in Trento, Italy, November 15–18, 2006.

18. Drayton, "Everyone a Changemaker," 8.

19. H. Grant and L. Crutchfield, "Creating High-Impact Non-Profits," *Stanford Social Innovation Review* (Fall 2007): 32–41.

20. D. McGray, "The Instigator," *New Yorker* (May 11, 2009).

21. "Philanthrocapitalists in Philadelphia; Arne Smiles," http://schoolsmatter.blogspot.com/2009/05/philanthrocapitalists-in-philadelphia.html.

22. McGray, "The Instigator."

23. National Center for Social Entrepreneurs, http://www.missionmoneymatters.org.

24. Bendell, *Lifeworth Annual Review of Corporate Responsibility*.

25. P. Anthrop, "Business Discipline and the Take-Charge Leader," *Nonprofit Quarterly* (Summer 2008): 72–73.

26. "Planned Parenthood's New Approach Draws Critics," *Chronicle of Philanthropy* (June 23, 2008), http://philanthropy.com/news/philanthropytoday/5009/planned-parenthoods-new-approach-draws-critics.

27. M. Shuman and M. Fuller, "The Revolution Will Not Be Grant-Funded," *Shelterforce Online*, no. 143 (September/October 2005); B. Weisbrod, "The Pitfalls of Profits: Why Nonprofits Should Get Out of Commercial Ventures," *Stanford Social Innovation Review*, vol. 2, no. 3 (Winter 2004).

28. The *Washington Post* piece is cited in http://www.theglobalreport.org/issues/229/environment.html; see also B. Jones, "Citizens, Partners or Patrons? Corporate Power and Patronage Capitalism," *Journal of Civil Society*, vol. 3, no. 2 (2007): 159–77; R. Mosher-Williams, ed., *Research on Social Entrepreneurship: Understanding and Contributing to an Emerging Field*, ARNOVA Occasional Paper 1, issue no. 3 (2006).

29. L. Rodriguez, "The Girl Scouts: Uncharted Territory," *Nonprofit Quarterly* (Fall 2007): 22.

30. S. Strom, "Dissent Inside Habitat for Humanity," *New York Times*, January 9, 2008.

31. Cited in C. Chetkovich and F. Kunreuther, "Social Entrepreneurship and Social Justice: A Critical Assessment," *GIVING: International Journal on Philanthropy and Social Innovation* (2009).

32. R. Dart, "Being Business-like in a Non-Profit Organization: A Grounded and Inductive Typology," *Non-Profit and Voluntary Sector Quarterly* 33, no. 2 (2007): 290–310.

33. A. Conner and K. Epstein, "Harnessing Purity and Pragmatism," *Stanford Social Innovation Review* (Fall 2007): 61–65.

34. M. Edwards, *Civil Society* (Cambridge: Polity Press, 2009).

35. T. Skocpol, *Diminished Democracy: From Membership to Management in American Civic Life* (Oklahoma City: University of Oklahoma Press, 2003).

36. H. Boyte, "Virtual Forum on the Civic Engagement Movement," 2007.

37. P. Eisenberg, *Challenges for Nonprofits and Philanthropy: The Courage to Change* (Lebanon, NH: Tufts University Press, 2005).

38. W. K. Kellogg Foundation, *Blurred Boundaries*.

39. J. Collins, *Good to Great in the Social Sectors* (New York: HarperCollins, 2005).

40. E. Frazier and K. Hall, "United Way's Challenge," *Charlotte Observer*, August 27, 2008. See also N. Jagpal, "Nonprofit Executive Compensation: Who Decides What Is Fair and How?" National Committee for Responsive Philanthropy, Washington, D.C., July 3, 2008. The CEO in question was later fired by her board.

41. C. Piller and D. Smith, "The Give and Take for Charity," *Los Angeles Times*, July 7, 2008.

42. J. Morgan, "Study Finds Nonprofit Leaders More Effective Than Corporate Heads," *Nonprofit Quarterly*, January 7, 2008, http://www .nonprofitquarterly.org.

43. E. Schwartz, "Venture Philanthropy: A Report from the Front Lines," in *Venture Philanthropy 2002: Advancing Nonprofit Performance Through High-Engagement Grant-Making* (Reston, VA: Venture Philanthropy Partners, 2002).

44. Seedco Policy Center, *The Limits of Social Enterprise*.

45. M. Koivusalo and M. Mackintosh, *Health Systems and Commercialization: In Search of Good Sense* (Geneva: UNRISD, 2004).

46. L. Garrett, *Betrayal of Trust: The Collapse of Global Public Health* (New York: Hyperion, 2000).

47. R. Wade, *Governing the Market: Economic Theory and the Role of Government in East Asian Industrialization* (Princeton: Princeton University Press, 2003).

48. D. Johnston, "2005 Incomes on Average Still Below 2000 Peak," *New York Times*, August 21, 2007.

49. Vision of Humanity, Global Peace Index, http://www.visionofhumanity. org/gpi/results/rankings/2008.

50. O. James, *The Selfish Capitalist* (London: Vermilion, 2007).

51. D. Callahan, "The Moral Market," *Democracy Journal* (Summer 2009): 49–59.

52. R. Wilkinson and K. Pickett, *The Spirit Level: Why More Equal Societies Almost Always Do Better* (London: Allen Lane, 2009).

CHAPTER 4

1. From Alan Krueger's introduction to the Bantam edition of *The Wealth of Nations* (New York, 2003).

2. ReasonOnline, "Rethinking the Social Responsibility of Business: A Reason Debate Featuring Milton Friedman, John Mackey and T. J. Rodgers," http://www.reason.com/news/show/32239.html.

3. J. Speth, *The Bridge at the Edge of the World: Capitalism, the Environment, and Crossing from Crisis to Sustainability* (New Haven: Yale University Press, 2008).

4. Cho, "Politics, Values and Social Entrepreneurship," 37.

5. G. Cross, *An All Consuming Century* (New York: Columbia University Press, 2002).

6. E. Malkin, "New Commitment to Charity by Mexican Phone Tycoon," *New York Times*, June 28, 2007.

7. D. Brook, "Triumph of the Wills," *Nation*, November 16, 2007.

8. Bornstein, *How to Change the World*, 269–70.

9. Cited in Chetkovich and Kunreuther, *Social Entrepreneurship and Social Justice*.

10. T. Watson, "Jeff Skoll's Changing World," *Huffington Post*, April 5, 2007.

11. Drayton, *Everyone a Changemaker*.

12. S. Sinha, "Silicon Valley Development Paradox," 2007. Unpublished op-ed.

13. R. Nilekani, "Philanthropy, Old and New," *Hindu*, July 13, 2008.

14. Cited in *Social Enterprise*, vol. 3, no. 25 (2004): 7.

15. "Charity Begins in Washington," *New York Times* editorial, January 22, 2008.

16. "Update Public View of Charity," Third Sector, June 26, 2007, http://www.thirdsector.co.uk; National Survey of Giving and Volunteering in the United States, 2008, http://www.independentsector.org.

17. GuideStar International, http://www.guidestarinternational.org.

18. New Philanthropy Capital, http://www.philanthropycapital.org.

19. Impact Reporting and Investment Standards, http://iris-standards.org.

20. GiveWell, http://www.givewell.net. A. Kamenetz, "When the Giving Gets Tough," *Fast Company*, April 11, 2008.

21. Collins, *Good to Great in the Social Sectors*, 1.

CHAPTER 5

1. M. Lee, "Paul Farmer Throws Fireballs and Gets a Standing O," Social Edge, http://socialedge.org/blogs/berkeley-bottom-line-2008/archive/2008/03/29 (accessed August 2, 2009).

2. D. McGray, *The Instigator*.

3. J. Rauch, "This Is Not Charity," *Atlantic Monthly*, October 2007.

4. A. Vance, "A Software Populist Who Doesn't Do Windows," *New York Times*, January 11, 2009.

5. SustainAbility, *Growing Opportunity: Entrepreneurial Solutions to Insoluble Problems* (London: SustainAbility, March 28, 2007).

6. P. Brest, "NCRP at Its Most Presumptuous," *Huffington Post*, March 5, 2009.

7. National Committee for Responsible Philanthropy, http://www.ncrp.org.

8. See chapter 2, note 21.

9. M. F. Gates, "Remarks to the Annual Conference of the Council on Foundations," Seattle, 2007.

10. P. Harris, "They're Called the Good Club—and They Want to Save the World," *Observer*, May 31, 2009.

11. S. Strom, "Age of Riches: Big Gifts, Tax Breaks and a Debate on Charity," *New York Times*, September 6, 2007.

12. D. McNeil, "Gates Foundation's Influence Criticized," *Los Angeles Times*, February 16, 2008.

13. Carnegie UK Trust, http://www.carnegieuktrust.org.uk.

14. P. Dietz, "This Is What Philanthropy Looks Like," Social Actions, July 18, 2008. http://my.socialactions.com/profiles/blogs/2062983:BlogPost:3523.

15. A study from Indiana University puts "Public-Society Benefit" giving at 8 percent of overall giving in 2008, http://www.philanthropy.iupui.edu/News/2009/docs/GivingReaches300billion_06102009.pdf; Resource Generation, "How Much Funding Goes to Communities of Color?" 2007, cited at http://www.resourcegeneration.org/Resources/giving_race_stats.html (accessed August 3, 2009); *Social Justice Grantmaking: A Report on Foundation Trends* (New York: The Foundation Center and Washington, D.C.: Independent Sector, 2005).

16. Cited in S. Worthington, president of InterAction, "Testimony Before the Senate Foreign Relations Subcommittee on International Development and Foreign Assistance," June 12, 2007.

17. Cited in C. Fishman, *The Wal-Mart Effect* (London: Penguin, 2007), 219.

18. Resource Generation, http://www.resourcegeneration.org.

Index

About the Author

Michael Edwards is widely recognized as one of the world's leading authorities on civil society, philanthropy, and social change. For the past thirty years, he has worked to strengthen the contributions of ordinary citizens to their communities as a grant giver, writer, advocate, organizer, and activist across five continents, and has lived and worked in Zambia, Malawi, Colombia, India, the UK, and the United States.

Michael graduated from Oxford University with a "congratulatory" first-class honors degree in geography, and was awarded a Ph.D. by the University of London for his work on housing the urban poor in Latin America. Dissatisfied with academic research, he entered the world of nongovernmental organizations (NGOs) in 1982 and spent the next fifteen years as a senior manager in international relief and development NGOs, including Oxfam GB, Save the Children UK, the Prasad Foundation, and Voluntary Service Overseas.

During this time, Michael became known for his innovative thinking about NGOs and development, and in 1998 he was invited to join the World Bank in Washington, D.C., as a senior adviser on civil society, where he led a program to improve the agency's engagement with a wide range of nongovernmental groups. Two years later, he was appointed as director of the Ford Foundation's Governance and Civil Society Program in

New York, overseeing grants totaling more than $900 million between 1999 and 2008, when he left to become a distinguished senior fellow at Demos, a Network for Ideas and Action, in New York; a senior visiting scholar at New York University's Wagner School of Public Service; and a senior visiting fellow at the Brooks World Poverty Institute at Manchester University in the UK. Michael also cofounded the Seasons Fund for Social Transformation, which makes grants to voluntary organizations that combine their work for social justice with spiritual principles. He is a trustee of the Center for Contemplative Mind and Society in Northampton, Massachusetts.

Michael is the author of thirteen books and hundreds of articles and op-ed pieces, and his writings have changed the way we think about voluntary action and the transformation of society. He writes regularly for openDemocracy, the *Financial Times*, the *Chronicle of Philanthropy*, and many other newspapers and magazines, and is a featured speaker at literary festivals and other events around the world. He lives with his wife, Cora, a nonprofit–fund-raising consultant who also teaches at New York University, in Swan Lake, a small community in the foothills of the Catskill Mountains of New York, where they have painstakingly rebuilt and renovated one of the first houses built by settlers who arrived in the 1830s to establish a tanning industry in Sullivan County. You can visit Michael's Web site at http://www.futurepositive.org.

Dēmos

Dēmos is a non-partisan, public policy, research and advocacy organization founded in 2000. Headquartered in New York City, Dēmos works with advocates and policy-makers around the country in pursuit of four overarching goals:

- a more equitable economy with widely shared prosperity and opportunity;
- a vibrant and inclusive democracy with high levels of voting and civic engagement;
- an empowered public sector that works for the common good;
- and responsible U.S. engagement in an interdependent world.

DEMOS FELLOWS PROGRAM

Dēmos is proud to be part of a progressive movement that is reshaping the way new ideas inform the public and policy debates, operating on a basis of shared responsibility and shared progress. We are working to incubate and execute new and diverse solutions to shared problems, and to offer long-range goals that can create stability and prosperity for Americans and people around the world. Through the work of the Fellows Program, Dēmos supports scholars and writers whose innovative work influences the public debate about crucial national and global issues. The program offers an intellectual home and public engagement platform for more than 20 fellows from diverse backgrounds: emerging public intellectuals, journalists, distinguished public figures, and academics whose research can be used to inform the policy world.

connect at Demos.org

eUpdates | Research, Commentary & Analysis | Special Initiatives & Events
Ideas & Action Blog | Twitter, Facebook & News Feeds | Multimedia

About Berrett-Koehler Publishers

Berrett-Koehler is an independent publisher dedicated to an ambitious mission: Creating a World That Works for All.

We believe that to truly create a better world, action is needed at all levels—individual, organizational, and societal. At the individual level, our publications help people align their lives with their values and with their aspirations for a better world. At the organizational level, our publications promote progressive leadership and management practices, socially responsible approaches to business, and humane and effective organizations. At the societal level, our publications advance social and economic justice, shared prosperity, sustainability, and new solutions to national and global issues.

A major theme of our publications is "Opening Up New Space." They challenge conventional thinking, introduce new ideas, and foster positive change. Their common quest is changing the underlying beliefs, mindsets, and structures that keep generating the same cycles of problems, no matter who our leaders are or what improvement programs we adopt.

We strive to practice what we preach—to operate our publishing company in line with the ideas in our books. At the core of our approach is *stewardship*, which we define as a deep sense of responsibility to administer the company for the benefit of all of our "stakeholder" groups: authors, customers, employees, investors, service providers, and the communities and environment around us.

We are grateful to the thousands of readers, authors, and other friends of the company who consider themselves to be part of the "BK Community." We hope that you, too, will join us in our mission.

A BK CURRENTS BOOK

This book is part of our BK Currents series. BK Currents books advance social and economic justice by exploring the critical intersections between business and society. Offering a unique combination of thoughtful analysis and progressive alternatives, BK Currents books promote positive change at the national and global levels. To find out more, visit www .bkcurrents.com.

Be Connected